JOSEPH & RUTH

JOSEPH & RUTH

'A CLASSIC COMBINATION'

DERICK BINGHAM

AMBASSADOR

Belfast Northern Ireland Greenville South Carolina

JOSEPH
© 1986 Derick Bingham
First published 1986
This edition June 1999

RUTH
© 1992 Derick Bingham
Amidst Alien Corn 1972
This edition June 1999

ISBN 1 84030 055 8

Ambassador Publications
a division of
Ambassador Productions Ltd.
Providence House
16 Hillview Avenue,
Belfast, BT5 6JR
Northern Ireland

Emerald House
1 Chick Springs Road, Suite 203
Greenville,
South Carolina 29609, USA
www.emeraldhouse.com

JOSEPH

CONTENTS

$\mathcal{I}$NTRODUCTION

WE ARE SURROUNDED CONSTANTLY WITH THE TENSION BETWEEN REALITY AND VISION. DRIVE INTO ANY LARGE city early in the morning when there is snow on the ground and there are the joggers making we car-bound people feel lazy as they run through slush and ice with a vision of fitness in their heads and the reality of a freezing morning on their faces.

Look at that little child in your house full of eagerness and joy at its first toy or bicycle and I'll guarantee as a parent you often wish that child never had to face the grim reality of a world filled with pornography, blasphemy, poverty, selfishness, war, division and plain old trouble.

I've had my dreams bruised by reality, often, but I don't see why I should give them up. I never found any joy in mere mediocrity. The bruising heals in time, anyway, and is replaced by a glorious itch! Of course reality and vision create tension but where there is no vision the people perish.

I live in a city where we don't need to go looking for trouble, it comes looking for us, but, I have proved that a vision for something better than things as they are can actually become a reality. No one proved it better than Joseph. The dreamer became the governor: the visionary became the emissary: the mentor became the Saviour: the captive became captivating. Let me prove to you just how captivating he became.

Derick Bingham
Summer of '86

'*Happy families are all the same: every unhappy family is unhappy in its own way.*'

LEO TOLSTOY

REALITY FIRST

GENESIS 37: 1-11

THE BIBLE IS A BOOK THAT DOES NOT WAFFLE. GRAPHICALLY, CAREFULLY AND WITH REALITY IT TELLS us the details of Joseph's family background. It does not make pleasant reading.

Joseph's father was a cheat, a con-man, as slippery a deceiver as ever drew breath. In turn he was conned by his father-in-law into marrying the wrong woman, and, when he married the right one the jealousy and connivance between the two makes even television soap opera plots seem mild. And I don't recommend most television soap operas I've seen.

When the children came the plot thickened. Rape, heartless cruelty and incest stained their lives as brother after brother lived for themselves and the devil. To put a fine point on it the children of Israel were plain, downright hoodlums.

Into such an environment what was arguably the godliest of all young men in Scripture was born. Few were to equal him in character, perception and consistency. If ever a child was born for his times Joseph was that child. He was to leave a mark for God which the sands of Egypt or the aeons of millennia cannot erase. His influence was to stretch from an Egyptian Pharaoh's palace to your heart and mine in this nuclear age. Young people by the million have had their hearts gripped by his rise from obscurity in doing the will of God in an Egyptian prison to becoming the epitomy of godliness to countless generations of believers down through the centuries: an epitomy that inspires, encourages and dares others to follow the sound of the distant drum to which he responded. Joseph's life says 'Don't just dream it – be it!' But notice that the reality comes first. His background was frightening.

Are you discouraged by your background? You were raised in no 'school of the prophets', you live amongst a crowd of miserable, selfish, conniving people. Perhaps your parents are divorced, your brothers and sisters smoke pot and your relatives are more interested in money and material gain than their spiritual standing. They would rather gain the whole world and risk losing their own souls. What chance have you got to live for God, keep your mind and life clean and do good? You have repented of sin and trusted the Saviour but you feel out-numbered and powerless. Others have godly homes, a healthy local church to attend and lots of Christian friends. You come from a house where the word godly was never heard of, go to a church which is anything but healthy and is sick, if not already dying: you would be glad to see a Christian's dog around, never to speak of a Christian! I recently met a college professor's wife who told me her son was the only professing Christian in one thousand pupils at his high school. Things were lonely for the lad.

Things must have been lonely for Joseph too. When reading through Joseph's family background recently I honestly wondered why some of the gory detail is given, and, if you think the word gory is slang, read Genesis 34! The answer now appears to be very clear to me. The detail is given because God is setting out the reality of where Joseph came from so that we can appreciate what His power and love can make a young life become, despite its background, if only that young life will respond to Him.

All over the world I meet people who are bitter about their backgrounds or position in life. 'If only this ... if only that', they moan. You would be surprised how folk think. 'If only my nose were a different shape. If only my Dad drove a Porsche. If only my brothers were kind, I would be kind too.' Never, in pursuing the life of Joseph do I ever read that Joseph ever said 'If only my uncle Esau had not been an outdoor type who cared only for the immediate rather than the eternal. If only...'

The reality of the awfulness of Joseph's family and background only shows more clearly the greatness of the God in whom he put his trust. Let me categorically state that I care not what your background, how dark your circumstance, how wicked your relatives, how thin your wallet, how lacking your opportunities for earthly advancement, how obscure your ambition to put God first may seem: God says 'Those who honour me, I will honour'. It may not mean success in earthly terms: for Joseph it meant first a pit and then a prison but always remember that it was into this background of unmentionable evil that Joseph was born and from which a vision of great things arose. The same can happen in your life.

'No dream comes true until you wake up and go to work.'

ANON.

$\mathcal{D}$REAMING $\mathcal{O}$F $\mathcal{T}$HINGS $\mathcal{T}$HAT $\mathcal{N}$EVER $\mathcal{W}$ERE

GENESIS 37: 1-11

BEFORE WE STUDY JOSEPH'S DREAMS IN ANY DETAIL I FEEL IT IS IMPORTANT TO STATE THAT I AM NOT building a systematic theology on the interpretation or mystery of dreams.

God spoke to the Joseph of the Old Testament in two dreams when he was but a teenager, and God spoke through a dream to the Joseph of the New Testament when he was moving towards marriage. God spoke to Pontius Pilate's wife through a dream and in one of the most famous incidents in Scripture God spoke through a dream to Jacob as he lay sleeping with his head on a rock pillow. Obviously God used this method according to His divine will.

Because God used dreams to speak to those folk does that mean that every time we have a dream we should wake up in a sweat and stay in a sweat until God shows us what the dream meant? Obviously such a situation would make our lives a prisoner of our dreams. It could even lead us into the bondage of the occult. The fact is we now have the written Word of God as our sole rule of faith and everything we do, waking or sleeping, must be weighed against it. Too many false cults have arisen in this world based on 'The-Lord-spoke-to-me-in-a-dream' syndrome. Besides, it is a plain medical fact that too many prawns can make you dream and I am, for better or for worse, very prone to prawn cocktails!

Joseph's dreams were used of God to speak to him and God can still use dreams to speak to people but what He uses in the dream to speak to them never contradicts the truth of His written Word. Joseph's dreams were undergirded by the promise of God to Abraham. God had promised Abraham that his seed would be preserved and now that seed was about to be threatened by a great famine. Joseph dreamt that as his brothers were binding sheaves of corn in the field one day his sheaf stood upright and his eleven brothers' sheaves made obeisance to his sheaf. His second dream involved the sun, moon and stars making obeisance to him. These dreams were saying that Joseph was to become great in his family and time was to prove that he was to become great in order to preserve life. God's covenant with Abraham was to be kept through Joseph. So it is clear that any dream out-of-line with God's Word or promises is suspect and he or she is a fool who tries to build anything substantial on it. But let me balance this with a personal story.

One morning I had the privilege of broadcasting God's Word on the BBC with our local church. In the course of the message from God's Word I quoted Samuel Rutherford's lovely statement that it was no foolish thing for a drowning man to cast himself on a rock neither was it a foolish thing for a drowning man to cast himself on Christ for salvation. An older man was listening who for most of his life had resisted the Gospel. That afternoon he went to sleep and dreamt he was drowning. When he woke up he remembered the broadcast and the statement of Rutherford and was awakened to his need of Christ. He was subsequently converted and on the day of his baptism rose out of the water, sat down on a seat and died. God still uses dreams but any use he makes of them neither detracts from nor does it add to His Word.

Dreams, of course, are always tempered with reality. Even projects that require vision and imaginative planning are bugged by limitations. In the 1960s the US President John F. Kennedy launched a very imaginative space program to put a man on the moon within a decade. It was defying history but Jack Kennedy said, "Some men see things as they are and say 'why?' I dream of things that never were and say 'why not?'"

On the day John Glenn blasted into space TIME magazine's White House correspondent Hugh Sidey was at the White House covering the occasion. What he got from the President was a roasting about the fact that his magazine had erroneously reported certain personal facts. Sidey profusely apologised. Kennedy profusely criticised him. When the President's secretary rang him to say that Glenn had splashed down and was on the line, Jack picked up the phone, glaring at Sidey: 'all right, stand there and see if you can get this right…' Then, after greeting the astronaut with an eloquent speech, he set the receiver down and began berating TIME once again. If you had heard that eloquent speech on radio or television you would never have guessed it had been surrounded by such an earthly problem seconds before it was spoken or seconds after millions had heard it.

Joseph had no sooner dreamt of things that never were, and shared it with his brothers, than he discovered the tension between vision and reality in full fury. His brothers erupted. The implication of eleven bowing sheaves bowing to Joseph's sheaf was not lost on them. Perverted though they were they got the message loud and clear and hated him for it. When Joseph shared his second dream of the sun, moon and eleven stars being subservient to him envy boiled in his brothers even more.

Up until this point in his life Joseph had been criticised for one upmanship in his behaviour. At seventeen he brought his father an evil report of his brothers and now he seems to be touting dreams of superiority. 'A tell tale, a bragging teenager' have been labelled on the lad. When his father made him a coat of many colours it certainly was no working coat for a shepherd: it was an unquestioned mark of favouritism. When the favoured son of Jacob comes not only wearing his coloured coat but speaking of dreams that seem to spell superiority, the family, never to speak of some Bible commentators, cannot take it. 'What is this dream that you have dreamed? Shall I and your mother and your brothers come to bow down ourselves to you to the earth?', questioned the doubting Jacob.

But can we blame Joseph for all the misunderstandings? Is it not wise, sometimes to warn of evil? Was Joseph just a 'tell tale' because he told his father of his brothers' evil doings? Just because the river is quiet doesn't mean the crocodiles have left. Warning is necessary but as Churchill discovered when he first warned of the rise of Nazism in Germany, it can get you sent into a wilderness by the mainstream of opinion at the time. Even in everyday life warning of, and exposing, evil is a very difficult road to walk. I remember so well as a prefect at school being tested on this issue. Indiscipline was rampant on the school bus and it was fellow pupils who were involved of my own age and upper sixth level. I felt it my duty to tell and the culprits were punished by the Headmaster. I was 'sent to Coventry' by some in my own class and called for everything but the indiscipline stopped. I cringe even yet at the thought of what it cost me. How easy it would have been to keep quiet and let it go. Later in my life how glad I was when a loving hand reached out and saved me from personal disaster by some straight talking. Now in middle life, I watch evil rampage even in local churches and good men keep silent and discipline breaks down. The testimony in the eyes of the on-looking world is akin to salt that has lost its savour and when salt loses its savour in the Middle East it is used to make roads on which people walk. They do the same on Christian salt that has lost its savour. But salt smarts and so does uncontaminated Christian salt. Look at what Mary Whitehouse has taken from 'The Establishment' for trying to apply the law of Britain to the standards of playwrights and television producers! I watched her defend moral and Christian truth one evening on television as an ordained clergyman tried to make her look foolish. I felt ashamed of my own cowardice so great was her courage. It's a well worn cliché but still very true that any old dead fish can go with the stream but it takes a living one to go against it. Don't be too hard on

Joseph for telling his father of the evil which was abroad in his family. It showed moral courage and any person showing moral courage will be 'in for it' from any immoral crowd.

And what of Joseph's sharing of his dreams? Was it bragging? Do the Scriptures say so? Certainly not. It may have been naïve but it was no sin. The naivety of youth is such that it does not understand the envy, jealousy and hatred that fills those who are older. How can it? It does not have enough experience. Have you ever met anyone who wanted to be a teenager again? Teenage naivety is one of the most vulnerable things in the world.

The 'in word' in the Church of Christ in the West at the moment is the word 'sharing'. Maybe we don't share enough of our problems and heartaches with each other but one thing is certain, you'd be a fool to share all the secrets of your heart with others. Hezekiah did that with the treasures of the temple at Jerusalem when some Babylonian visitors called: the result was that those visitors came back a few years later with an army and took all his treasures away and the people with them. Watch who you share your secrets with because another person's secret is like another person's money: we are not as careful with it as we are with our own.

Always keep in mind that Joseph's dreams were God given, both times. The fact that God spoke once, even twice, and Joseph's family did not perceive it was not Joseph's fault. Again and again we shall see similarities between Joseph and the life of Christ. Is not this the very first one? Did not Mary berate her twelve year old son for staying in the temple instead of coming home with her? Was it arrogance on the part of our Lord to remind her of higher priorities marked out for Him? None of Christ's immediate brothers or sisters accepted or believed in Him when He began His ministry. Did not the Saviour say that He had come to His own and His own had received Him not? He was not deflected from the path of obedience by His family and, as we are about to learn, neither was Joseph. Neither should we. It is no sin to dream of things that never were and say 'why not?'; especially if those dreams are God given. The exciting thing was Joseph's dreams were going to come true. So can yours.

FAVOURITISM BREEDS DIVISION

GENESIS 37: 12-36

'FATHER'S DAY,' THE SMALL BOY POINTED OUT, 'IS JUST LIKE MOTHER'S DAY ONLY YOU DON'T NEED TO SPEND so much!' A father has been defined as someone who carries pictures where his money used to be. 'The trouble with a parent is that by the time you are experienced, you're unemployed', said another and Peter Ustinov commented that, 'Parents are the bones on which children sharpen their teeth!'

Someone once asked a good question: 'Wouldn't it be wonderful to be as brilliant as our children thought we were when they were young and only half as stupid as they think we are when they are teenagers?'

Parenthood is no easy task whatever its definition and one of its deadliest traps is when a parent shows favour to one child above another. It is such an easy trap to fall into and Jacob fell right in. There can be no doubt that Joseph was his father's favourite and there were understandable reasons for it. Was not Joseph the firstborn of the only woman Jacob ever loved? Rachel was a stunningly beautiful woman and no doubt her son inherited a lot of her good looks. Now that Rachel was dead Joseph was a constant reminder to his father of the woman for whose love he had laboured fourteen years. They had seemed as a day to Jacob so great was his love for Rachel. Now her son was his link with the past and he showed deference to him. It was a luxury he should not have allowed himself.

Jacob as a parent was not a good manager. In any marriage the husband should be a good manager, not doing everything and making every decision himself, but keeping an eye on everything that is happening and moving in to help or advise where it is needed. Jacob must have ignored the jealousy his favouritism aroused for, when Joseph's brothers saw that their father loved Joseph more than any of them 'they hated him and could not speak peaceably to him'. Surely Jacob was not deaf. He must have chosen to ignore the conversations around him.

It is so easy to indulge in what seems a legitimate luxury which, in your heart, you know to be playing with fire. Favouritism fuels jealousy so deadly it can kill. You think I exaggerate? Joseph's brothers very nearly got around to killing him because of what their father had created in their hearts by his behaviour. Watch that look of deference in your eye, that touch, that planning and those gifts towards your children. If you don't, long after you are gone, that look, that touch, that plan, that gift will rancour in the heart of those who were not deferred to.

When Jacob sent the seventeen year old Joseph to Shechem, alone, he was behaving very irresponsibly. With the reputation his brothers had and the memory of the disgusting actions of former days when they had been in Shechem in his mind, how could Jacob have sent an innocent seventeen year old to find out how they were? Little did Jacob think that as Joseph left him to go to Shechem he would not see his son again for twenty-two years.

Has your father sent you on an errand which has got you horribly mixed up in a swirl of events that threatens to destroy you? Maybe he did such a thing thirty years ago and it still rancours in your heart. I'm quite sure Joseph didn't relish the idea of approaching his brothers alone and away from home. If his brothers couldn't speak reasonably to him at home what would they not do if they got him far from his father? Yet, Joseph said nothing to his father which he would later regret.

I shall never forget a young man coming to see me one day about the unreasonable behaviour of his father towards him. He poured out his story, words tripping upon words as he told me the havoc his father was causing in his life. I identified with his hurt and agreed that his father's behaviour was most unreasonable but slowly there arose in my mind a feeling that I should warn him. (It came from a line I once read in one of Frank Boreham's books asking what if the person receiving the spiteful letter you have just written were dead by the time your 'I'll-set-him-right' letter arrived?) Gently I pleaded with the anxious chap in my study not to say anything to his father which he would regret as he might have to stand, God forbid, at his father's graveside. He promised not to say anything hurtful but to wait for God to unravel His plan for his life. I am no seer, nor the son of one, either, but the very next morning his healthy father slumped dead. Ashen faced that young man returned to thank me for having warned him of the dangers of berating an unreasonable parent. He told me to share his story with others if I felt it would help.

The Scripture speaks of a man finding Joseph wandering in a field in Shechem. Poor Joseph! I think, I can see him there in that field, unable to find his brothers and maybe, in his heart, wishing he wouldn't. Enthusiasm is always easier than obedience but Joseph obeyed his father. Again there are shades of the Saviour in Joseph. The Father's sending of His Son into the world was no irresponsible act but we see the Lord Jesus ask in Gethsemane, 'Father if it be possible let this cup pass from me'. It was not possible and in obedience he faced the jealous men who shouted for his blood and the cruel hands that tore His robe from Him and into the pit of death He went for us. Obedience, though it seemed to bring disaster, actually brought incalcuable reward: Joseph was to learn this principle as few have done.

As Joseph lay in the pit, due to Reuben's intervention, I'm quite sure he didn't shout, 'Praise the Lord, don't you fellows know I am to be Governor of Egypt and free you one day from death and starvation! This pit is marvellous because it is the actual highway of God's guidance for me!' No pit of suffering in our lives ever appears to be the path to blessing. Joseph thought he was merely doing his duty and suffering for it. So it is in all matters of guidance: let us do the legitimate duty of today, no matter what it costs and God will use it to lead us on to greater things. After all, the will of God for me is to do the legitimate duties of today. 'Do as the occasion serves you', said Samuel to Saul and it was good advice.

But what could Joseph do as he lay in the waterless pit? He looked broken beyond repairing. Gone was the coat of distinction, gone was home support, gone was every visible means of help. Just like you? Hemmed in? You can't go back and you can't seem to go forward?

To underline what favouritism had done in their hearts the Scripture emphasises that Joseph's brothers then 'sat down to a meal'. They munched food while their brother lay helplessly in a nearby pit! Heartlessness is a friend of jealousy and envy is the root of every sin we commit against our brethren. As some Ishmaelites passed by an idea springs into Joseph's brothers' minds: why not sell Joseph? The passing traders are first called Ishmaelites to show their origin and then Midianites to show where they came from. For twenty shekels of silver Joseph is sold to the descendants of the cast-out son of Abraham by the grandchildren of the chosen son of Abraham, Isaac. Ironic, isn't it? How were those despised Ishmaelites to know that the lad they carried to Egypt was one of the greatest young men the world was ever going to see? God was not going to bring good out of the evil of Jacob's favouritism or his eleven sons' burning jealousy for there never was any good in evil at any time. Good was going to be brought in spite of the evil. But the warnings against favouritism and jealousy come like beacons from this story to us today. Let us despise favouritism and jealousy like a plague. Israel and his children were to be sorry they didn't.

'If you decide to make thrills your regular diet ...
they will get weaker and weaker, fewer and fewer,
and you will be a bored, disillusioned old man for
the rest of your life.'

C. S. LEWIS

ℋer ℋouse ℐs ℱhe ℱay ℱo ℋell

GENESIS 39: 1-20

'FOR AT THE WINDOW OF MY HOUSE I LOOKED THROUGH MY LATTICE AND SAW AMONG THE SIMPLE, I PERCEIVED among the youths, a young man devoid of understanding ... passing along the street near her corner ... he took the path to her house ... with her enticing speech she caused him to yield, with her flattering lips she seduced him. Immediately he went after her, as an ox goes to the slaughter, or as the fool to the correction of the stocks, 'til an arrow struck his liver. As a bird hastens to the snare, he did not know it would take his life. Now ... listen to me ... pay attention to the words of my mouth: do not let your heart turn aside to her ways, do not stray into her paths; for she has cast down many wounded, and all who were slain by her were strong men. Her house is the way to Hell'.

The quotation is from the wisest man in all the earth. He wrote hundreds of proverbs and none are more powerful than his proverb about the house of the immoral woman. Tragedy was that Solomon went into her house himself and the wisest man in all the earth became one of the earth's greatest fools.

Joseph was never tempted to go into her house. He had a far greater temptation to face: he worked there. Sold by the Ishmaelites to Potiphar, one of Pharaoh's officers, a captain of the guard, it was not long before Potiphar was aware that his slave was no ordinary slave. 'His master saw that the Lord was with him and that the Lord made all that he did to prosper in his hand. So Joseph found favour in his sight and served him. Then he made him overseer of his house and all that he had he put into his hand ... and Joseph was handsome in form and appearance.'

The scene is all too familiar. Our biggest test is not when people criticise us or persecute us or when things are difficult; our biggest test comes when we are successful. Again and again when a person does well they forget God and the success that turns their head usually wrings their neck. Not so Joseph. His greatness was to be highlighted in the house of Potiphar as never before. Success in the world's terms usually means increased sales, high profitability and promotion but success in the Bible often means the very opposite. Loss of popularity, loneliness and misunderstanding chase after the doer of God's will like a bloodhound. Joseph was about to become successful in God's eyes.

The devil has no difficulty in making sin look innocent for the devil is usually good looking. The Bible says so. The subtlety of his attack on Joseph came through the eyes and words of Potiphar's wife. The Scriptures pinpoint her approach; 'Now it came to pass after these things that his master's wife cast longing eyes on Joseph and she said, "Lie with me".' The look that swept over Joseph was calculated and a look can say in a second what ten thousand words could not convey as powerfully in an hour. Note that the look proceeded her words: do we have any idea of the impression a look can give?

I obviously cannot speak for a woman's viewpoint but I can for a man's. There is a very helpful statement in the Bible from the one who is arguably the greatest believer in history. Some would claim that he had no written Scripture to comfort him and certainly his circumstances seemed to contradict the promises of God because he had lost his business, had been horrifically bereaved and his health was gone. His faith held despite his circumstances but he became the taunt of young men.

'And now', said Job, 'I am their taunt song ... I am their byword. They abhor me, they keep far from me; they do not hesitate to spit in my face ... they pursue my honour as the wind, and my prosperity has passed like a cloud.' (Job 30).

Despite the taunts around him Job defends his honour with a little phrase every man could do with having as his motto: 'I have made a covenant with my eyes; why then should I look upon a young woman?' (Job 31:1).

Here was Job telling us the secret of overcoming in the area of immoral behaviour: he had made a promise to keep his eyes pure. Let every man (including the writer) reading these words make the same promise with his eyes. With pornography in virtually every newspaper shop in the land, flaunted from late night and even mid-day television films and on virtually every advertising hoarding, it will be one of the best promises you ever made. It will not be an easy promise to keep.

Recently I was in a restaurant with a friend when three men came in and sat at a table near us. They would not give over annoying a young woman who was serving at the tables. I could stand it no longer: 'Leave her alone, lads', I pleaded.

'So he has a higher standard than us!' one mocked, and, looking at the chicken on my plate, threatened, 'I'll come and stuff that chicken down your throat.' Circumstances fortunately did not go that far but they left the young lady alone and later left the restaurant. 'We nearly had stuffed chicken for lunch!' quipped my friend as he set out for home. Indeed!

Joseph's opposition to sin was ten thousand times more difficult. Potiphar's wife spoke to Joseph day after day, tempting him. 'Look,' he said, 'my master does not know what is in the house, except through me, and he has committed all he has to my hand. There is no one greater in this house than I, nor has he kept anything back from me but you, because you are his wife. How then can

I do this great wickedness and sin against God?' Daily insistent temptation is much harder to resist than a 'one off' temptation. But Joseph resisted for the Lord's sake. Many a person would give in if temptation and opportunity came together but the powerful combination did not reach Joseph. When she 'caught his garment', pleading with him, 'he left his garment in her hand and fled and ran outside.'

Three things bring down a lot of men; greed, glory and girls. None of them destroyed the godly son of Jacob. By God's grace he overcame by refusing sin point blank. There was no dallying, even before being faced with her crowning attempt the Scriptures tell that 'He did not heed her, to lie with her or to be with her.' In every possible circumstance he avoided her. When that became no longer possible, he ran for it.

But lust has a side-kick called hate. What first appears as a sweet smelling rose has thorns which pierce. The woman's disappointed passion whipped around and used Joseph's garment as a case against him. First she called in the men of her house and lashed out at her husband, 'See he has brought in to us a Hebrew to mock us.' To speak in such a way about her husband in front of others certainly indicates that all was not well in her married life. Watch the woman who criticises her husband in front of others: it indicates that there is trouble behind closed doors. Then the woman drew on a weapon which millions have used down through the centuries with increasing vehemence: anti-semitism. Joseph now became 'this Hebrew slave'. There was a hiss in her voice on the word 'Hebrew'. When her husband came home she used it again: 'This Hebrew servant whom you brought to us came in to me to mock me', she lied.

A recent book by Martin Gilbert entitled 'The Holocaust' documents with frightening accuracy the anti-semitism of Europe in this century. I thought it was bad until I started reading this book and then I discovered it was almost as Hell let loose. I defy anyone to read this book and remain unmoved as he documents the history of men and women using anti-Jewish feeling to cover their own lust for power and dominance. The sad thing is that such behaviour is as old as the story of Joseph.

Potiphar was angry when he heard his wife's accusations against Joseph but it is not an indication of Potiphar's high regard for Joseph that he only placed him in prison instead of commanding his execution? Perhaps he did not give much credit to her story and put Joseph in prison because he must be seen to do something.

Surely the most outstanding thing at this point in Joseph's story is Joseph's silence. Not a word of defence or explanation from Joseph is recorded in Scripture. A word might have saved him but no word is given. Into prison he goes without a personal protest.

As the doors shut upon Joseph we almost hear the words of his brothers echoing along the walls: 'We shall see what will become of his dreams!' Let all the modern teachers who present doing the will of God as being accompanied by outward success come alongside Joseph in prison and see how they can get around this situation. People often say, 'He got that job, it was an answer to prayer', 'She got better, it was an answer to prayer', 'They eventually got married, it was an answer to prayer.' What if he didn't get that job? What if she didn't get better? What if they both remained single until death? Would these be answers to prayer too? We are all too success orientated. Let's learn from this episode that should we even be imprisoned because of some liar and only God is glorified in our loneliness that is incalculable reward in itself.

'Two men looked out through prison bars,
one saw mud and the other stars.'

ANON.

$\mathscr{T}$HE $\mathscr{M}$ASTER $\mathscr{O}$F $\mathscr{D}$REAMS

GENESIS 40

THE SURGEON ALWAYS MOCKED. HE MOCKED HIS YOUNG ASSISTANT VIRTUALLY EVERY TIME HE HELPED him perform an operation. He curled his sarcasm into a phrase which came to haunt the young man. Five stinging, searing words seemed to sum up what the young fellow judged to be the truth, though he had no affection for his superior. What were they? 'You'll never be a surgeon'.

Years later Dr. A. J. Cronin was called to an isolated woodsman's home in Scotland on a freezing snow-bound day. A tree had fallen on the woodsman and his injuries were multiple causing paralysis and he needed immediate surgery. Dr. Cronin got him to the local hospital by the sledge and tried to phone Glasgow to get the injured man to a surgeon as he felt totally inadequate to carry out the required operation. The telephone lines were down. Undaunted Dr. Cronin tried to get the local station master to get a message via the railway network. No trains were running.

Dr. Cronin was in a corner. He looked at the anxious faces of the young family around him and at the body of the woodsman before him and suddenly there arose in his mind the words he had heard years before that now seemed to clap in his ears like thunder. They said: 'You'll never be a surgeon.' He weighed the words and he scanned the anxious faces and then made his decision. He operated. A few months later the young woodsman walked out of that Scottish cottage hospital.

Another phrase had been curled at Joseph, 'We shall see what shall become of his dreams', said the children of Israel. What they had failed to realise was that when God gives a gift to anyone he doesn't give it in order to later ignore it. God makes sure that the gifted person is also given the sphere in which to exercise their gift. Even a prison can become a platform for a gift to emerge; even for a master of dreams.

Joseph's circumstances were hard but the fact that his own position was the result of injustice made no difference to the faithfulness and loyalty with which he carried out his duties. The keeper of the prison did not look into anything that was 'under Joseph's hand because the Lord was with him; and whatever he did, the Lord made it to prosper.' Men of the world are not slow to detect real character and to take advantage of it.

The night was a perpetual rainstorm in a small town in the United States when an older man and his wife turned in to a hotel looking for a room. The young manager had no rooms to spare but he gave up his own to the older couple for the night. One year later the manager received a round trip ticket to New York from the older man and on arrival was taken to the sparkling Waldorf Astoria hotel in mid-town Manhattan. The older man turned out to be the owner of the hotel and had been on the look out for a good manager. He reckoned he had found his man on a rainy night in a small town and his man took the offered post on the spot!

It was not North America and it was not in the Waldorf Astoria but it was a prison in Egypt and the two men brought into custody one day were very high ranking figures in Pharaoh's palace: the chief butler and the chief baker had offended their master and had been put into the charge of the captain of the guard: the Scriptures say, 'In custody in the house of the captain of the guard, in the prison, the place where Joseph was confined.' Potiphar's house was obviously adjoined to the prison or was part of the same complex. Immediately Potiphar put Joseph in charge of these men. Such an action seems to further prove that Potiphar didn't believe his wife's story about Joseph.

These two men lay down one night and both of them dreamed memorable dreams which by the next morning had affected the very look on their faces. 'Why do you look so sad today?' said Joseph.

It says a lot about Joseph that he cared enough about the men he served to ask why they were sad. If anybody seemed to have a right to sadness it was Joseph. Nobody asked him how he felt; nobody enquired about his mood. It was obvious that Joseph wanted to cheer them up. His thought was all for the others. Here was another shadow of his Lord touching the edge of his life for was it not the prisoner on the Cross who washed His disciples feet and who, in the agony of pain, later made provision for the care of His mother? Was it not another prisoner who showed such Christ-like qualities when dragged up from his cell, manacled with chains, to appear before the fascinated King Agrippa? How does he address him? 'I think myself happy, King Agrippa...' are his opening words. Happy, indeed! The Saviour's words can be epitomised in the prisoners of conscience in the Bible: 'he that saveth his life shall lose it and he that loseth his life for my sake shall find it.'

Alexander Solzhenitsyn said that he discovered, when he was a prisoner of conscience in Soviet prisons that the only people in the prison who were truly free were the believers! Joseph proved that to be true even in his day.

Joseph's fellow prisoners explained that they seemed to have dreamed uninterpretable dreams. Like a flash Joseph turned their attention to God. He didn't say 'Have you heard about my gift, fellows? You have come to the right man!' Instead Joseph said, 'Do not interpretations belong to God? Tell them to me please.' God got the glory. As Vance Havner put it: 'The man who thinks he is too big for a little place is too little for a big place.' Joseph did not despise his lowly position, he just gave God the glory in every situation. The results were to be far reaching.

No sooner had the butler told his dream than Joseph gave him the interpretation, coolly, calmly and accurately: 'Within three days Pharaoh will lift your head and restore you to your place.'

But then came the human plea, the first indication of how Joseph really felt in his heart about all his experiences. 'But remember me when it is well with you and please show kindness to me; make mention of me to Pharaoh and get me out of this house. For indeed I was stolen away from the land of the Hebrews: and also I have done nothing here that they should put me into the dungeon.'

It is a very human touch: 'Make mention of me to Pharaoh. Get me out. I am homesick and a victim. I am innocent.' Is there a hint of trying to nudge providence, here? All of us try to hurry things along but God will not be hurried. Joseph has two more years of preparation left before he would see the end of his prison experience. He has to learn, thoroughly, before he is given great responsibility that God's timing is always perfect. His very human desire to get out of prison was to be subservient to God's timing. Joseph's hopes went with the chief butler but he 'Did not remember Joseph but forgot him.' Our hopes are often pinned on this person or that, but when will we ever learn that people are as fickle as the weather and often change with their circumstances? Only God is unchangeable. Only His promises can be trusted. If God wants you out of where you are He will take you out, unmistakably. You don't need to build up 'contacts', you don't need people in 'high places', you have the highest friend in the universe, you are accepted in Him and you have nothing to fear. He can use just whatever He chooses to accomplish His will for you. Surely that is the most important thing.

A burning bush for Moses. A stalled star in the sky for Joshua. A fleece for Gideon. A jaw bone for Samson. A corn field for Ruth. Fire from heaven for Elijah. A floating axe head for Elisha. A lump of figs for Hezekiah. A raised golden sceptre for Esther. A burning coal for Isaiah. Yokes for Jeremiah. The fingers of a man's hand for

Daniel. A great fish for Jonah. A vision of a red horse standing among myrtle trees in a hollow for Zechariah. A coin in a fish's mouth for Peter. A blinding light on the Damascus road for Paul. A vision of the future on a prison island for John.

All of these were used to guide each of these individuals at some point in their lives. It teaches us that we need not lean on the arm of chance, we need not cultivate the world's public relations systems in order to be heard. When God opens a door, no man can shut it. But the emphasis is on the word 'When'. Joseph's door was not to be opened for two more years.

It took a lot of moral courage for Joseph to give the chief baker the interpretation of his dream but Joseph did not baulk at telling him the truth. In three days the chief baker would be dead.

As Joseph waits for God we now see qualities which were to mark him all down the line as more than a dreamer. Here was ability without instability. Here was attractiveness without vanity. Here was cheerfulness without lightness. Here was gift without lording. Here was courage without rough handling. Here was godliness that was as real to the man as breathing. Here was what seemed to be a water carrying, floor scrubbing skivvy who was soon to govern a nation. Here was someone who did not wait for some great occasion but who made every occasion great.

'Very often a change of self is needed
before a change of scene.'

A. C. BENSON.

GETTING READY FOR CHANGE

GENESIS 41

THERE WAS TROUBLE ON THE THIRTY-EIGHTH FLOOR.
THE WALLS HAD SHOWN A CRACK AND THE ARCHITECT
was called. He immediately took the escalator to the basement. The
basement? Of course! If there is trouble at the top of a building then
the architect wants to know what's going on at the foundations.

Slowly and carefully the foundations had been laid in the life of
Joseph. He was learning that God's time was wisest, that God's grace
was sufficient; all the foundations were to be tested on a scale Joseph
could not have imagined. His rise to power was initiated by God in
the mind of a man who was asleep. Strange? Not so strange! Did not
Adam get his wife when he was fast asleep? A Pharaoh sleeping
was now God's instrument in bringing Joseph's gift before the world.
Incredible, yes, but incredibly true.

Pharaoh dreamed twice. The first dream was of seven fat and
seven thin cattle; the gaunt cattle ate up the fat ones. The second
dream was of seven thin heads of grain devouring full heads. His
spirit was troubled when he awoke and he sent for 'all the magicians
of Egypt and all the wise men.' That surely must have meant

a tremendous crowd. It was not until every one of them had failed to interpret Pharaoh's dream that the chief butler remembered Joseph and spoke of Joseph's phenomenal gift for interpreting dreams.

Two years seemed a long time from Joseph's interpretation of the butler's dream to Pharaoh's hearing of him. Notice God's timing. The long wait had managed to bring about a comparison between Joseph and every wise man in Egypt in the presence of Pharaoh. What human manipulation could ever have brought such a wonderful thing about?

I once had guidance from God about something I was sure I must do for Him in the future but it was a full six and a half years and journeyings that took me literally around the globe and back home over the North Pole before it started to come to pass, one foggy evening. You may have to wait many years before your vision is fulfilled. Remember Zacharias? When the angel told him that Elizabeth was to have a baby, Zacharias thought God had forgotten all about their prayers. God waits to fulfil His promise to you and when the last jig-saw piece in your circumstance fits, you will see that it is done with incredible skill. You will yet worship.

'Then Pharaoh sent and called Joseph and they brought him hastily out of the dungeon: and he shaved, changed his clothing and came to Pharaoh.' I could be accused of sentimentality but when I read such a line it always makes me want to cry. Somehow the pathos in the sentence is a world of its own. One can almost see the slave-prisoner shaving and preparing himself for his first appearance at Pharaoh's palace. Pharaoh's minions are standing in the background urging him to hurry. He turns toward the open door, a door to fame and spiritual fortune which is to influence the history of the world. The door would close and hurrying feet would ascend, never to return to that prison house again. Pharaoh's throne room was to echo to those feet from now on. It was a great moment. The sheer God's-in-His-heaven-and-all's-well feeling about it! God's will is costly, heart renderingly difficult but I tell you, my much burdened Christian friend, the door will one day open for you too and you shall see the King of Kings.

The principle Joseph proved can come true for you: 'See a man diligent in his business? He shall stand before Kings.' A call may one day come to represent your Lord in the corridors of power in the country where you live. May you be found as faithful as the man who shaved himself and changing into new clothes moved out into a new day of service for God.

The first words of Pharaoh were a door of opportunity for Joseph to show off his gift. 'I have heard it is said of you that you can understand a dream to interpret it.' Would Joseph succumb to the temptation to say, 'Sure, no problem, you have got the very one you need!'? The long years of preparation for this moment were not wasted. The whole history of Israel hung upon how Joseph would answer and, as in his prison days, so now in his stupendous moment of destiny, he did not fail. 'It is not in me; God will give Pharaoh an answer of peace.' Joseph let Pharaoh know even before he attempted to answer the question of Pharaoh's dreams, where the source of his gift lay. The humble Joseph gave God the glory again in his life and the courts of Heaven rang with the joy of it. If there is one sentence that sums up Joseph's attitude to all the fame he was to be given it is encapsulated in that little phrase 'It is not in me.'

Pharaoh proceeds to tell Joseph of his dreams and without any hesitation Joseph proceeds to give the interpretation. He explains that seven good years are to be followed by seven lean years in Egypt and that Pharaoh's two dreams were actually one and was 'Repeated to Pharaoh twice because the thing is established by God and will shortly come to pass.' Joseph advised Pharaoh to select a discerning and wise man to be set over Egypt to collect one fifth of the produce of the land in the seven good years, to be stored in the cities in order that food would be in reserve for the seven years of famine that would follow.

No hint was given by Joseph that he was the best man for the job! Not a word of connivance passed his lips. He gave the interpretation of the dream and the practical application and left the results with God. Can we not do the same in our lives? Let us do the will of God and leave the far reaching repercussions with Him.

Whether you raise children, teach school, run a corporation, captain a submarine or man a check-out desk, do it to the glory of God.

First it was obeying his father in going to see how his brothers were getting on, then it was the oversight of Potiphar's house, then the oversight of the prison and now it was the oversight of Pharaoh's house and the nation of Egypt: Joseph had learned to do everything to the glory of God. 'You shall be over my house', said Pharaoh, 'and all my people shall be ruled according to your word … see, I have set you over all the land of Egypt.' Pharaoh took off his signet ring and gave it to Joseph, he gave him fine linen clothes to wear and a gold chain around his neck. If there had been registration on chariots Joseph's would have read 'No. 2'. People were to bow down to Joseph everywhere he went and to sum it all up Pharaoh said, 'Without your consent no man may lift his hand or foot in all the land of Egypt.' It was all far away from a dry pit in Shechem but it all came together within a few minutes of a humble plea which said, 'It is not in me'. May God help us to talk like Joseph!

Not in me to lift the weary spirit
Not in me to save a precious soul,
Not in me to make a day seem brighter,
Not in me to set a nation's goal.

Not in me to move a congregation,
Not in me to heal a broken land,
Not in me to tell the secrets of the future,
Not in me to turn the tide upon life's sand.

Not in me to bring about repentance,
Not in me to put life into bones,
Not in me to bring about revival,
Not in me to calm ten thousand moans.

Not in me to be a new trail blazer,
Not in me to write the inspiring song,
Not in me to stop the gossip's story,
Not in me to halt the critic's tongue.

All in Him the power to change a nation,
All in Him to break the Satanic sword,
All in Him for love and life and future,
Jesus Christ, my Master, King and Lord.

As the thirty year old Joseph now moves into his new work for God the first thing he is given is a new name 'Zaphnath-Paaneah'. 'Nath' has in it the idea that 'God speaks and lives'. The second event in his life, and, next to his relationship with God, the most important thing, was the woman with whom he was going to spend his life. It is not good for a man to be alone and through Pharaoh, Asenath is given to Joseph.

It is important to remember that this event was before the laws of Moses were imposed on the children of Israel regarding marriage and it is quite clear that Joseph did not allow the pagan background of the daughter of Poti-pherah, priest of On, to influence him. Joseph remained a monogamist all his life, for, this is God's ideal in marriage. In a society famous for its harems Joseph stayed by Asenath and their marriage was a solid foundation for the massive work he was about to accomplish. 'There are a few things,' said Jobyna Ralston, 'that never go out of style, and a feminine woman is one of them.' Asenath proved to be just that for Joseph.

The first child to be born to this very happy couple was called Manasseh meaning 'God has made me forget'. In his naming we learn for the first time the significance of the hurt Joseph had borne internally over all those years. The silence, the lack of bitter complaint, the patience with which he faced wrong doing was outstanding but the naming of Manasseh proved the cost, mentally, to the long suffering Joseph. Joseph's mind was being healed of all he had come through. It is great to learn that God can make us forget the hurts in our lives by the comforts He sends. A little child can be used by God to do that like nothing else can. The trust and affection of a little child is a very precious thing: it is a sacred trust. The past of a father's life is unknown to the infant and the pain associated with events long gone never crosses its mind. 'Now!' is the word for infants and not 'Yesterday'. God soon healed Joseph's memories.

His second son was called 'Ephraim' meaning 'God has made me fruitful'. As the years of plenty came in Joseph 'gathered very much grain as the sand of the sea, until he stopped counting, for it was without number'. Joseph's life was full and Ephraim was named to mark the reality of all the blessing that God had sent.

'I do not pray for a lighter load but for a stronger back', said Phillip Brooks. That stronger back for the load ahead was about to be given to the father of those two little boys. The famine soon hit Egypt in all its fury and 'the people cried to Joseph for bread'. The test had come and Pharaoh said to all the Egyptians, 'Go to Joseph: whatever he says to you, do.'

The parallel between Joseph and the Lord Jesus comes again in our story, beautifully and clearly. Before we close this chapter and move on to study what was happening all this time to Joseph's family let us just trace once again the parallels between Joseph and his Lord and as we do let's not be afraid to make this point in this book a time for worship.

Who was the morning star? Joseph. Who was the sun who followed? Jesus. Who maintained moral purity in the face of severe and daily temptation? Joseph. Who did no sin neither was deceit found in his mouth? Jesus. Who suffered under a lie? Joseph. Who was crucified on the testimony of false witnesses? Jesus. Who had two fellow prisoners, one raised to a new life and the other to death? Joseph. Who was crucified in the presence of two thieves one who went to Paradise and the other to perdition? Jesus. Who suffered the depths of humiliation and rose to be far above all? Jesus. Who became the saviour of a nation? Joseph. Who became the Saviour of the world? The Lord Jesus Christ. And I promise you, if you keep reading, there's more, much more.

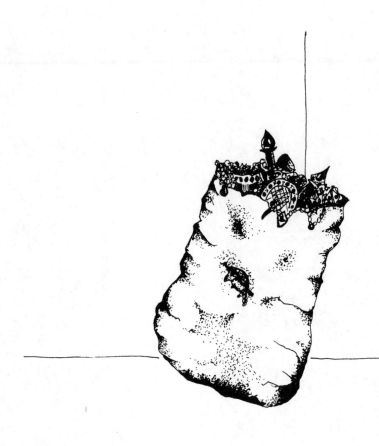

'Cowardice asks, "Is it safe?" Expediency asks, "Is it politic?" Vanity asks, "Is it popular?" Conscience asks, "Is it right?"'

W. M. PUNSHON

MORE THAN A DREAM

GENESIS 42

'OH YES', SAID THE INDIAN, 'I KNOW WHAT MY CONSCIENCE IS. IT IS A LITTLE THREE CORNERED THING in here,' – he laid his hand upon his heart – 'that stands still when I am good: but when I am bad it turns around and the corners hurt very much. But if I keep on doing wrong, by and by the corners wear off and it doesn't hurt anymore.'

The sons of Jacob must have had a lot of corners worn off in the decades that followed their wicked action, yet, God's grace reached out to them through a famine. One day their father heard that there was grain in Egypt and as his family faced starvation he ordered his sons to go to Egypt. 'Go down to that place and buy for us there, that we may live and not die', he said. The very word 'Egypt' triggered a floodtide of memories in those sinful minds. 'Why do you look at one another?' asked Jacob. Little did he know the circumstances behind those looks. It was the awakening of conscience.

Ten of Joseph's brothers set out for Egypt and never did ten men have a more salutary journey. Every turn of the road must have reminded them of the young seventeen year old they had sold into slavery. The circumstances had now drastically changed. Does someone identify closely with this part of the story? Are you walking in your day and generation, the path Joseph had to take? The crowds despise you for it. Mark my words: they will need you before you will need them. Who would ever have imagined that the slave of the Midianites entering Egypt decades before was now the most powerful figure in the whole famine stricken Mediterranean – North Africa region? Could you ever imagine that those who despise you and say all manner of evil against you could ever come to you for help? Life will hold great surprises for you, just wait and see.

Who are those figures bowing themselves down before Egypt's Governor with their faces to the earth? They are the mockers! Who is that great personage whom they have now been brought to for grain? He is the dreamer! To the letter God's promise was fulfilled. It was all truly more than a dream. Joseph, suddenly recognising his own brothers 'remembered the dreams which he had dreamed about them'. It must have been one of the most momentous moments of his life. But his brothers didn't recognise Joseph. Obviously he had physically changed between seventeen and thirty eight and together with his Egyptian language they simply didn't associate their brother with the great person before them. One thing is certain: when God promises, He delivers, for recognise Joseph or not they had just bowed the knee to their brother.

We now come to one of the most difficult parts of the story of Joseph to interpret but yet there are very practical lessons to be learned from it. The Scriptures show that Joseph acted as a stranger to them and spoke roughly to them. 'You are spies!', he said. Was Joseph acting out of character? Was he being vindictive? The answer seems clear as the story develops: Joseph was testing his brothers to see what kind of characters they now possessed. If there was not improvement in them then he must bring it about.

'We are twelve brothers', they pleaded, 'the youngest is this day with our father ... and one is no more.' How easy it would have been for Joseph to snap, 'That's what you think!', but note the reserve, the patience of Joseph. He could have displayed his power in a great sensational scene. It reminds us of Joseph's Lord when two Greeks enquired of His disciples saying, 'Sirs, we would see Jesus.' He did not give in to Israel's stubbornness and say 'Right! If you are not interested in me, the Gentiles are. I'll display my power to them!' Rather he pointed out that his first duty was to the 'lost sheep of the house of Israel'. Joseph's first priority was the repentance of his brothers and he believed that the longest way round was the shortest way home.

Joseph demanded that Benjamin be brought to him as proof of his brothers' story, one would fetch him and the rest would be imprisoned until he arrived. 'So he put them all together in prison three days.' After three days Joseph released them and commanded that one be imprisoned while the rest would take grain to their home and then return with Benjamin.

The animated conversation that followed showed that their consciences were now fully awakened. 'We are truly guilty concerning our brother for we saw the anguish of his soul when he pleaded with us and we would not hear therefore this distress has come upon us.' Joseph then turned away and wept. Here was a man with social prestige, financial authority and royal privileges, crying. A normal man would have rejoiced but this was no normal man, this was a spiritual giant. The man of the world would have said, 'You all deserve it. Too right you are about the reason for this distress coming upon you!' but Joseph turned away and cried. In all of his career Joseph was never stronger than the day he first wept over his brothers. Those tears showed a great heart. God forgive us if we ever gloat when God vindicates us. Joseph was so sure footed in all his reactions both in days of distress and in victory. He was more moved by God's goodness to him in bringing about this amazing turn of events than he was in any motivation of spite against his brothers.

Simeon was chosen to remain in Egypt and now the perceptibly changed men headed back to Canaan, only to find the money they had used to pay for their grain was returned in each of their sacks! Is it any wonder the Bible comments that 'their hearts failed them'? But even under pressure the men were different to the men who had first left home to buy the so desperately needed grain. In their language Joseph was now no longer 'the dreamer', but he had become 'our brother' and 'the child'. When they spilled out the story of their adventures to Jacob, this time there were no lies.

Jacob's reaction was very typical of him. 'You have bereaved me of my children: Joseph is no more, Simeon is no more and you want to take Benjamin away. All these things are against me.' There was not a word or sign of trust in God in Jacob's language, not a promise of God quoted, not a breath of hope but just whining and misery. He claimed everything was against him while, if he had only realised it everything was for him!

We can all be just as blind. We look at life around us and whine, all the time forgetting that, although everything that happens to us is not good, God is making sure that it works together for good. The very moment we think everything is against us is the very moment everything is working out for us if we had only the trust in God to realise it. Maybe I could express it all more succinctly in a poem:

Just as he was having his toughest day,
And Goliath was coming with a lot to say,
And Israel was silent, come what may,
God was working it out for good!

Just as they thought it would never come,
And three walls surrounded Babylon,
And the people of God were sick for home,
God was working it out for good!

Just when the times were dark and dread,
And the Assyrian hosts by a fiend were led,
The angel moved and the foe lay dead,
God was working it out for good!

MORE THAN A DREAM

Just when they thought their case was lost,
They heard a knock and said 'It's a ghost,'
But Peter arrived when they needed him most,
God was working it out for good!

Just stop today and bow your knee,
Though you're ready to scream and ready to flee,
Lift your heart to him and say with me,
God is working it out for good!

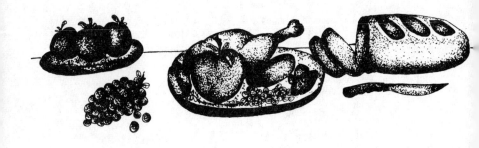

'People will not care what you know until they know that you care.'

ANON.

Don't Write Them Off

GENESIS 43

THERE NEVER WAS A CHILD SO ATTRACTIVE, SO INTELLIGENT, SO LOVING BUT HIS MOTHER WAS GLAD to get him asleep! As a parent, maybe, those days have long since passed for you. Childhood passed so quickly to teenage years when those children of yours no longer wanted to put their shoulders to the wheel, all they wanted to do was get their hands on it! Maybe that stage is also passed and some weary eyes read these words that have long wept over a son or daughter who did not stop at cars. The quarrels have stopped. The kitchen door slamming is over. The threats have ceased. You have given up. Your son has moved out. Your daughter has long eloped. All that remains is silence and a lot of memories.

You could be in for a big surprise. Take Judah. The history of this Bible character was most unsavoury. He was so immoral and careless that his daughter-in-law tricked him into thinking she was a prostitute in order to have children. She had twins by him and in any family such a character would not have had a chance of honour or a hope of even becoming anything. That is, apart from the grace of

God. It was Robert Louis Stevenson who said, 'There is nothing but God's grace. We walk upon it; we breathe it, we live and die by it; it makes the nails and axles of the Universe.' Grace turns monsters into men, social climbing women into social blessings and jealous and spiteful teenagers into inspiring leaders. A drop of God's grace is worth an ocean of man's favour. Let's watch that grace at work in Judah.

Jacob, at this stage in our story just will not let Benjamin go. What poison is to food, self pity is to life. Self pity is when you begin to feel that no man's land is your very own island. Jacob had lashed out all around him with his tongue, blaming others when he was to blame himself. He wanted sympathy and the word 'Me' figured prominently in his thinking. You know how it is. You tell someone you have a pain in your shoulder and they reply, 'I had that once and was off work for six weeks!' You mention that your child has a sprained ankle and they reply, 'My child did that to his ankle last year and the doctor said it was the worst sprained ankle he had ever come across.' You mention that you had a few mishaps on your holiday and that opens up an hour's description of what went wrong on their holiday this year, last year, and you make a speedy retreat before year three is described! Self pity can blind you to the immediate needs of others and can isolate you. Jacob was certainly isolated but he was snapped out of it, not only by reality but by the surprising intervention and speech of his son Judah, of all people.

Judah pleaded with his father. He brought the awesome reality of the famine situation home to his father's mind and heart. He reminded him of the uncompromising Governor of Egypt. He asked to be trusted. He said he would take the blame for ever if he did not bring Benjamin back. It was a different Judah to the man who had sold his brother to the Ishmaelites. It had been Judah who had initiated the sale, and, says the Bible, 'His brothers listened to him.' That such wise and kind language should now pour from the lips of Judah was incredible. If there was hope for a Judah there is hope for anybody.

It is interesting that Jacob sent expensive presents to Egypt along with double the money his sons had just paid for grain plus the money they had found in their sacks. Money and 'balm and honey, spices and myrrh, pistachio nuts and almonds', all of these might touch the Governor. 'And may God Almighty give you mercy before the man, that he may release your other brother and Benjamin.' He certainly kept his options open, didn't he? He was soon to learn that the Governor of all Egypt was not interested in his money or his gifts: all he cared about was helping Jacob.

On arrival in Egypt the sons of Jacob were under the same delusion when they were taken to Joseph's house to dine with him. Fear gripped them for they thought, as they put it, 'We are brought in so that he may seek occasion against us and fall upon us to take us as slaves with our donkeys.' I find that amusing, don't you? Knowing what we know now about the whole story it seems ridiculous that they thought Joseph was after their donkeys! The most influential man in all Egypt brought them to his home to make them slaves and impound their donkeys! They may have sold Joseph as a slave but he neither wanted them as slaves nor did the wealthy Joseph want their donkeys. In life we often make a big thing out of nothing. Our fears are sometimes full of sheer paranoia. Even the steward of Joseph's house said, 'Do not be afraid. Your God and the God of your father has given you treasure in your sacks.'

It seems amazing that the direct descendants of Abraham had to be reminded of spiritual things by what was probably a pagan steward. 'Your God is behind all this!', he was saying. I find it interesting and fascinating to watch people from the lands we once called heathen now returning to our shores to preach the gospel with power, and particularly, enthusiasm, to a people who have largely grown cold and indifferent to the greatest message in the world. The steward certainly knew the secret of his Master's power as he brought Joseph's brothers into Joseph's house and gave them water to wash their feet, and, nice touch, 'gave their donkeys feed'.

Once more Joseph emerges at this point as a beautiful picture of Christ, particularly in relation to the attitude of folk before and after they get to know the Saviour. Note that the men's conception of Joseph was so pathetic in comparison to what he really was. Joseph immediately enquires about their father's health and he has to find a place to weep when he sees his young brother Benjamin because his great heart is so moved at the very sight of him.

I am sure even at this point, Joseph would have loved to reveal all that he had in store for his own but they were not yet ready to take it. So, says the Scripture, 'He restrained himself'. Meanwhile he ordered food for them. He sustained them until the time would come when he could reveal his glory! When the men sat down at the table they were set before him in order of age and 'the men looked in astonishment at one another'. Joseph knew even the very minutest detail of their lives.

The fine detail of Scripture at this stage in Joseph's life story is certainly not there as a mere history lesson. Notice the detail about Benjamin. We are told that Benjamin got five times as much food as any of the others because Benjamin was the only son, apart from himself, who had been born to Rachel. The others, Reuben, Simeon, Levi, Judah, Issachar and Zebulun were born to Leah whom Jacob did not love and whom he was tricked into marrying. Dan, Naphtali, Gad and Asher were all born to surrogate mothers. Benjamin was the son of his father's love and was marked out for particular affection. All along Joseph had wanted Benjamin, his immediate family, before him. Now that he had arrived Joseph intended to keep Benjamin before him.

Our conception of Christ is also pathetic in comparison to what He is really like. At conversion we discover that we have a great Christ for our need. We discover that not only is He mighty to save but He is also mighty to feel. He can be touched with the feelings of our infirmities. There is more power to save, to strengthen, to inspire, to comfort, to encourage in the word 'Jesus' than in all the utterances of man since the world began. 'Why,' said H. G. Wells, 'Christ is the most unique person in history. No man can write a history of the human race without giving first and foremost place to the penniless teacher of Nazareth.' But just as Joseph must have

Benjamin before him, so must our Lord Jesus have His loved ones before Him too. Literally? Yes. Let me prove it to you.

A friend of mine, when a young lad, used to play a lot of hockey in the back garden of his house. One day he discovered that his brother was missing and found him in the front room of their house, with, of all things, a girl! This continued for quite a few nights and all this brother seemed to want was to have this girl before him. His brother did his best to persuade him that there were some far more important things in life than a girl. He was not to be persuaded! Even when she wasn't there her photograph was prominently displayed.

My friend uses the incident to remind people of the apostle Paul's great message to the Ephesian Christians. Paul teaches those believers that they were once 'Without Christ ... having no hope ... but now in Christ Jesus you who once were far off have been made near ...? If that were not enough Paul adds another vital truth! He says, 'God hath raised us up together and made us sit together in heavenly places in Christ that in the ages to come he might show the exceeding riches of his grace in his kindness toward us through Christ Jesus.'

From childhood I have always puzzled over that phrase of Paul's speaking of God making Christians sit together in heavenly places. What does it ever mean? It means that once a person receives Christ as Saviour they have immediate access to God's presence through prayer every day of their life. If people ask me if I'm sure of going to Heaven I reply that I go there every day! This is not metaphysics: this is the truth. Being 'seated in the heavenlies' literally means that the Christian comes before God, daily, through prayer. That is why God loves His people to pray. That is why God said to Ananias when He wanted to send him to encourage the newly converted Paul, Behold ... he is praying!' The most mind bending, heart thumping, spirit lifting truth of all is that He wants His people to be before Him forever. 'For the Lord himself will descend from heaven with a shout, with the voice of the archangel, and with the trumpet of God. And the dead in Christ will rise first. Then we who live and remain shall be caught up together with them in the clouds to meet the Lord in the air. And thus we shall always be with the Lord. Therefore comfort one another with these words.' Ah! There's more to this story of Joseph than first meets the eye. Praise God.

$\mathscr{T}$HE $\mathscr{T}$EST

GENESIS 44

THERE LIVES IN ULSTER A FAMILY CALLED GLASGOW AND THE HEAD OF THAT FAMILY WAS A MAN affectionately known as 'F.C'. This man had built up a large departmental store in the town of Newtownards and he had quite a few sons. One of them, a doctor, was in his father's shop one day whenever a man entered it looking for the doctor's brother who was a gifted preacher. 'Are you the Glasgow that preaches?' he asked him. 'No,' he replied, tongue in cheek, 'I'm the one who practises!'

There are millions of people across the world who say they have repented and trusted Christ as their Saviour: what is one of the biggest barriers to the hundreds of millions of others who haven't? There can be no doubt that the answer is that too many Christians do not practise what they preach. Let me very quickly add that I have often been among them. Piety from the teeth out is easy, but, William Jenkyn said, 'A rotten apple discovers itself on a windy day'. Let us repent of hypocrisy lest a windy day finds us out. The wind of testing certainly rose to try Joseph's homeward bound brothers.

With sacks full of grain they were not long out of the city of the Pharaoh's palace when suddenly Joseph's steward appeared on the scene. 'Why have you repaid evil for good?' he asked, accusing them of stealing his Master's silver cup. Their protest of innocence was vociferous and they demanded that if one of them were guilty then he should be executed and the rest would be slaves. The steward was not so harsh but agreed that if one had the cup he would become his slave. Imagine their exasperation when the cup was found in Benjamin's sack! They tore their clothes in exasperation.

Joseph, of course, had placed the cup in Benjamin's sack in the first place. The whole exercise was to test these men. How would they react to the situation? Would they do what they would have done twenty two years before: Benjamin would have become a slave and borne the blame for the rest of his life. They would have saved their own skin and the old father's reaction would not have come into their reckoning. Judah would have been the leader, no doubt. In fact the opposite happened and they all returned together to Egypt.

Joseph's tactics of testing were working and the hypocrisy of the past had now been replaced with sincerity and family concern, and Judah was the leader. In one of the most moving speeches in the Bible Judah steps forward to intercede for Benjamin before Joseph. Meanwhile Joseph was still in the palace. He had been waiting for the results of the test and, when his brothers returned, he was not disappointed.

If you have set out on some work for God, my friend, it will not be long before you are tested by God. God's fire of testing will test any hypocrisy. Recently I stood in the beautiful Castle Ward, my favourite of all Ulster's historic houses, as the guide told us of the beautiful treasures of the house. 'But see these pillars', she said, 'you think they are marble but they are not. They are wooden pillars which have been treated in such a way as to look like marble.'

'That "lady" above the mantelpiece there is a bust in marble and it takes four men,' she pointed out, 'to lift it down.'

I looked at the pillars and looked at the marble and my mind imagined fire raging in such a house and licking those pillars. It would not be long until the truth of their outward deception would be stripped to charcoal. So it was in the ancient Greek temples when the fire raged. Cracks filled in with wax to substitute for proper repairs would come crashing down.

In the New Testament the Lord of the churches sends His angels with letters to each of the seven of His local churches. Moving, revealing, sifting, warning, challenging, frightening, tough – but – tender, the letters to the seven churches sort out the hypocrites like no other letters have. They all face the test of the Lord's scrutiny.

'You have a name that you are alive,' he warns the church at Sardis, 'but you are dead.' The church at Philadelphia was in danger of losing its reward, the church at Thyatira was hiding immorality, the church at Pergamos was hiding false doctrine, the church at Smyrna was under testing and was encouraged to be faithful to death, the church at Ephesus was patient, persevering and unwearied in its work for God but it had a fatal flaw, 'I have this against you, that you have left your first love … repent or … I … will remove your lampstand from its place.'

It was to the Laodiceans that the most tender yet frightening letter was written. You say, 'I am rich, have become wealthy and have need of nothing and do not know that you are wretched, miserable, poor, blind and naked', said their Lord. 'Because you are lukewarm, I will spew you out of my mouth…' He warns. How must they have felt when they read such a letter? But notice the balance. The Lord gives them a positive alternative. 'I counsel you to buy from me gold refined in the fire, that you may be rich.' He adds that He is standing outside the door of the church knocking and if anyone in the church will open and let Him in they will be able to know His friendship and certainly be able to obtain His refined gold. Will we hear the same voice?

I didn't like it when I lost my job,
Quickly,
Nor did I relish failing my exam,
Finally,

That trouble that erupted in my life,
Personally,
Did not ease life's hurried pace,
Smoothly,
When illness came surging in,
Painfully,
I prayed for health for all my days,
Immediately,
But heard a voice come over to my heart,
Quietly,
'All this is refining fire, my son,
Definitely,
To give you gold to make you rich,
Eternally.'

God's gold or the world's is a question millions face. Let's choose God's and be spiritual millionaires. Thank God that the second time around Joseph's brothers chose wisely. Judah now had his finest hour.

Judah's confession that God had found them out is the high point of all Joseph's strategy. No word of God had ever crossed Judah's lips to date but now it comes: 'What shall we say to my Lord, how shall we clear ourselves? God has found out the iniquity of your servants.' Judah recognises that God was at work and confesses it. Immediately Joseph tests him again by offering him a way out. He would keep Benjamin but the rest could go. It opened the floodtide of Judah's heart. He pleads that such a thing would kill his father. He offers to take Benjamin's place as a slave 'for how shall I go up to my father if the boy is not with me?'

No Christian can hear Judah's irresistible speech without casting the mind thousands of years forward to one of the most favoured prophecies of Scripture, familiar to millions, 'But you, Bethlehem Ephratah, though you are little among the thousands of Judah, yet, out of you shall come forth to me the one to be ruler in Israel, whose goings forth have been from old, from everlasting.'

As Judah went surety for Benjamin so that tiny infant of Bethlehem Judah came in order to go surety for us. Shades of greatness fall upon the repentant Judah, it truly was his finest hour and it broke all Joseph's restraint in two until he could hold back his glory no more. Judah had passed his test and now came the reward.

'*More tears are shed in our theatres over fancied*
tragedies than in our churches over real ones.'

F. C. RIDEOUT

$\mathcal{A}$ $\mathcal{H}$EART $\mathcal{U}$NCOVERED

GENESIS 45: 1-20

A LADY APPROACHED ME ONE DAY WITH A COMMENT WHICH HAUNTS ME EVEN NOW WHEN I THINK ABOUT IT. Her husband had died and she told me that her Christian friends had said to her, 'You let the Lord down by crying so much.' I wish I could talk to her friends for with friends like that she could do with a change.

The world often worships the heathen doctrine of Stoicism and I want to categorically state that Christian teaching denies it at every turn. Here is some great hero, an athlete, a film star, a politician and some tragedy happens in their life. They stand in the graveyard at the graveside of some loved one or come out of hospital in obvious pain, or are interviewed about some tragic turn in their careers. The camera moves in and they show no emotion, no tears flow, they say, 'You win some you lose some' and the world thinks it is a sign of greatness.

Stoicism has had some very distinguished exponents through the years right from Cicero to the present day. They teach that nothing is within man's power except imagination, desire and emotion. By cultivating a detachment from the world outside and mastery over his reactions to the world's impingement upon himself, the Stoic can achieve freedom and happiness. In its early days it rigorously excluded (when practices by Marcus Aurcleus) pity, denied pardon and suppressed general feeling. Sin was simply an error of judgment rectified by a change of opinion. Whatever his or her position in life, even if a slave, the Stoic could be inwardly free. It ruled out obedience to a personal god.

Christian truth presents a very different story. It presents a Christ who stands by the grave of a friend and weeps and who stands over a city and weeps and who goes to a garden and with strong crying and tears battles through in prayer. He commands that His followers rejoice with those who rejoice and weep with those who weep. Stoicism is not countenanced.

Dr. M. R. de Hann once calculated that if all the tears shed in the world could be barrelled and poured into a canal such a waterway would stretch from New York to San Francisco. He maintained it would make a river in which barges could be floated. Few would doubt him.

God created human beings with a capacity to weep: it is one of the most important capacities a human being has. Research shows that people who lose their loved ones in death and who do not allow themselves to weep at some point are probably heading for some future emotional trouble. You have to weep to express grief and we must let people weep.

I once sat in a crowded church building where a lot of the world's media were present. There had been a great tragedy and many deaths. The minister rose to speak and could not for he broke down in tears as he spoke. Somehow, in an inexpressible way, we were all comforted.

We do not want to develop any false 'art of weeping' but tears can be a true test of what kind of a heart we have. There are seven different occasions recorded in Scripture where Joseph wept. Men are not supposed to weep much but here is the most powerful man in all Egypt, the Saviour of starving nations, the man whose dreams came true, and again and again, he weeps. What does it show us?

At the Keswick Convention I was once having breakfast with George B. Duncan and, between pieces of toast, he gave me one of the best outlines I have ever received on the book of Nehemiah. You remember that Nehemiah was the man who wanted to rebuild the walls of Jerusalem. 'He took it to heart,' said George, 'he wept. Then he took it to God; he prayed. Finally he took it in hand; he worked.' Notice that the whole project started with the man weeping.

How deeply do we take things to heart? We can shut up our hearts and nothing, not even the starving of Africa could move us. We will be the losers. Tell me what a man cries at and I'll tell you the kind of man he is. If a person sheds no tears for people in need now we will shed few tears when they are gone. I know it, I've seen it; haven't you?

'Tell me, Sexton, what do you think was the success of McCheyne's preaching?' said the man being shown around the famous young preacher's church building in Dundee. Taking him into the pulpit he said to the man, 'Weep, sir, and when there is a pool of tears around your feet you will have found the secret of Robert Murray McCheyne's preaching.'

Joseph's weeping on Judah's intercession for Benjamin was no quiet weep. He cried out, 'Make everyone go out from me!' So, no Egyptian stood with him while Joseph made himself known to his brothers. 'And he wept aloud and the Egyptians and the house of Pharaoh heard it.'

Why did he put the Egyptians out? He didn't want them to know of his brothers' past behaviour. There was no telling what the Egyptians might have done to Joseph's brothers had they found out what they had done to their hero. Such a discovery would have jeopardised the entire future of the coming nation of Israel. The wisdom of Joseph was just as astute when he was overwhelmed with emotion as when he was guiding a nation. He even protected his brothers when he was weeping.

Then the moment of moments came. Joseph revealed himself to his brothers. 'I am Joseph,' he said, 'does my father still live?' Notice the first reaction of his brothers was fear. 'His brothers could not answer him for they were dismayed in his presence.' 'Please come near to me', he said and proceeded to unveil his heart to them. Not a word of reproach was uttered, not a word of anger was spoken. He even urged them not to be grieved nor angry with themselves but rather to see God in it all. 'God sent me before you to preserve life ... it was not you who sent me here, but God.' No mention was made of his persecution at the hand of Potiphar's wife, no mention came of his prison experiences or how his gift had influenced his future. It was all of God, alone. He said it, believed it and lived it. 'Not you ... but God ... He has made me a father to Pharaoh, and lord of all his house, and ruler throughout all the land of Egypt.'

Not ashamed, in his high position of his father (is there anything more pathetic than someone ashamed of a father who has remained in a humble walk of life?), Joseph gives the commission to his brothers that they go home with the good news to their father. 'Tell my father of all my glory in Egypt ... and bring my father down here.' Joseph fell on the young Benjamin's neck and wept again and after kissing all his brothers he ordered the loading of their beasts and invited his brothers to bring all their own families to Egypt. 'For the best of all the land of Egypt is yours.'

Confession certainly led to transformation for the sons of Jacob. At Penuel, years before, the Lord had wrestled with Jacob, interrogating him. 'What's your name?' He said. 'My name is Jacob', came the confession. Jacob means deceiver and supplanter. 'From now on you will be called no more Jacob but Israel meaning prince with God.' Yet, I never read that Joseph had to have his name changed by the Lord. 'I am Joseph', came the words on which the future of Israel hung. In that name came forgiveness, healing, sustenance, security and hope. To be 'accepted in the beloved' was for those bunch of former hoodlums a privilege beyond all privileges.

'I am Jesus whom you are persecuting', said the Lord to the

rebel Paul. On bowing the knee to his Lordship Paul came in for a spiritual fortune and millions have done the same. Have you? If you have, not only are you 'accepted in the beloved' now, but, what is more, one day you will be absent from the body and present with the Lord. The word present implies the thought of being 'at home' with the Lord.

What is the implication of the two thoughts, 'present with' and being 'at home with?' asked an inquirer of the late Tom Richardson. 'Ah! That's easy,' he replied, 'there's many a time I've been present with a man but I have not been at home with him!' replied Tom. It will, as Jacob and his eleven sons were soon to discover, be a pleasure to be both.

'If you think that you know the Will of God
for your life ... you are probably in for a very rude
awakening, because nobody knows the Will of
God for his entire life.'

ELIZABETH ELLIOTT

$\mathcal{A}$ $\mathcal{Q}$UESTION $\mathcal{O}$F $\mathcal{W}$AGONS

GENESIS 45: 21-28

RECENTLY I AGONISED OVER GUIDANCE ABOUT A CERTAIN MATTER IN MY LIFE. I WAITED AND WAITED FOR God, and then I waited some more. No answer came so I decided I must do something about the matter. Yet, I knew in my heart God had held up on purpose and that I would be flying in His face if I acted without Him. So, I waited again, while going on with the work in hand. That very weekend in a busy airport, then after a message given on Scottish soil, and then from a midnight phone call from New Zealand I had my answer. All three incidents of guidance came without me having to lift a finger to bring them about.

Our God does things. He is not a denomination, a sect, a list of rules, a systematic theology. He is, without question, a living God who will prove to any submissive heart that He lives and moves and cares. He is full of surprises.

When Jacob caught sight of his returning sons, including Benjamin, his heart rejoiced but when they burst in with the thrilling, dazzling, splendid news that 'Joseph is yet alive, and he is Governor over all the land of Egypt', he fainted! The man had lived like a spiritual pauper for years when all the time he was rich beyond all counting because of God's grace and mercy in using Joseph's life to bring incalculable blessing to him! I know many a Christian (myself included) who lives like a spiritual pauper half time when all the time they are the sons and daughters of the King.

'Now therefore, being justified by faith we have peace with God, through our Lord Jesus Christ', said Paul. Do we even stop to think of what a priceless thing it is to have peace with God? I have seen tens of thousands climb a mountain, and some climb it barefooted, in order to have peace with God. When we asked one fellow on the mountain, with bleeding feet, why he was doing it he told us it was to obtain peace with God. 'But have you ever heard that Christ made peace through the blood of His cross?' we asked him. 'I never heard that before', he replied.

No need to climb mountains, wear shirts, mutilate the body, or any such nonsense; the price of redemption has been paid at the cross. Our heavenly Joseph has attained the victory and all who trust him have, immediately, peace with God, it is already made if you rest in Christ alone for salvation.

'Through whom also we have access by faith into this grace in which we stand,' adds Paul. Grace to stand! Peace means that the past war and enmity with God is over. Grace means that there is enough strength to face the present, no matter what it throws up. And the future? 'We rejoice in hope of the glory of God.' What a combination; 'peace', 'grace' and 'glory', 'past', 'present' and 'future'! To look at some professing Christians today who would think they were thrilled with these priceless possessions?

It was, says the Bible, the sight of Joseph's wagons which revived Jacob. Unfortunately it usually took the tangible to convince Jacob. He was not famous for his faith so God, in great patience, sent him tangible proof of his goodness. Joseph was guided to send 'ten female donkeys loaded with grain, bread, and food for his father', but the wagons carrying Joseph's brothers' provisions for the journey made the greatest impression on Jacob. Why? It is probable that in the area where Jacob lived such wagons were unknown and so their very strangeness impressed Jacob that something very different must have happened to bring such wagons to his home.

'It is enough,' said Jacob, 'Joseph my son is yet alive: I will go and see him before I die.' Is it not worth thinking about that those who have great faith in God do not need constant tangible evidence that God is taking an interest in them? A fellow like me needs constantly to see tangible results from preaching God's Word in order to know God is with me. I wonder how I would get on in the mission fields of North Africa or in a nation like Japan where less that one percent of a population of millions profess Christ? A missionary once took me to a Japanese graveyard. There were 35,000 Buddhist graves there, with their prayer flags flying and five Christian graves lay in a corner of that amazing place. It stunned me. When we get to heaven it will be the brave men and women who for, maybe forty years of their lives have struggled against great odds and the oppressive forces of Satan who will be greatly rewarded. They saw very few people won for Christ in their lifetime but they didn't need tangible evidence that God was working for them in order for them to keep working for God.

Paul lying cold and damp, without books to read or a friend to defend him in a Roman prison had little tangible evidence that God had blessed his lifework. All the Christians in Proconsular Asia had forsaken him. He desperately pleads with young Timothy in his last letter on earth to take up the baton and run in the Christian race. The faith once delivered to the saints is now delivered to Timothy to hand on. I cannot read the letter, as Handley Moule put it, 'for mist rising in my eyes.' Somehow the pathetic circumstances Paul was in as he lay there waiting for Nero to send his men to take him out of his cell and on to the great Ostian Way to be beheaded makes the letter all the more poignant. No well laden wagons from Nero's palace rolled up to Paul's door. No gifts from his family or friends abroad lifted his spirit. Why this very morning a heart warming friend of mine wrote me a letter to offer me the gift of an entirely new computer system to help me with my Christian work and asked me to confirm by phone if I wanted one! No fellow received a phone call from me quicker! No such aid came to the lonely Paul as he wrote his letters and he was the greatest Christian writer in history. His words were the very words of divine inspiration. Did he moan in such circumstances? Did he cry out for tangible evidence that God had better prove to him that He cared?

Not a complaint comes from Paul's pen as he lifts his mind by faith to the prospect that lay ahead of that executioner's sword and the cold prison in which he was held. Read and mark his words again.

'For I am already being poured out as a drink offering, and the time of my departure is at hand. I have fought the good fight, I have finished the race, I have kept the faith.

'Finally there is laid up for me the crown of righteousness, which the Lord, the righteous Judge, will give to me on that day, and not only to me but also to all who have loved His appearing.'

I am glad for Jacob and his sons that God proved to them with material gain that He cared but greater is the faith of men, women and young people who can trust God even though they gain nothing out of it but rather, materially and physically lose. 'Blessed are they that have not seen and yet have believed,' said the Lord Jesus. They are the more faithful ones.

> I wonder if he remembers,
> That dear old man in Heaven,
> The class in the old red schoolhouse,
> Known as 'The Noisy Seven'.
> I wonder if he remembers
> How useless we used to be,
> Or thinks we forgot the lessons,
> Of Christ and Gethsemane?
> I wish I could tell that story
> As he used to tell it then,
> I think that with Heaven's blessing,
> I could reach the hearts of men.

I often wish I could tell him,
Though we caused him so much pain,
By our thoughtless boyish frolics,
His lessons were not in vain.
I'd like to tell him how Harry,
The noisiest one of all,
From the mission fields of Shiloh,
Went home to the Master's call.
I'd like to tell him how Stephen,
So brimming with life and fun,
Now tells to the people of Asia,
The tale of the crucified One.
I'd like to tell how Joseph,
And Philip and Jack and Ray,
Are honoured among God's workers,
The foremost men of their day.
I'd like, yes, I'd like to tell him,
What his lessons did for me,
And how I'm trying to follow,
The Christ of Gethsemane.
Perhaps he knows already,
For Harry has told maybe,
That we are all coming – coming,
Through Christ and Gethsemane.
How many besides, I know not,
Will gather at last in Heaven,
The fruits of that faithful sowing,
But the sheaves are surely seven.

'If what they are saying about you is true, mend your ways. If it isn't true, forget it, and go on and serve the Lord.'

HARRY A. IRONSIDE

CHANGE

THERE IS AN OLD AND VERY BEAUTIFUL STORY OF A WOMAN WHO DREAMT THAT SHE SAW THREE OTHER women at prayer. As they kneeled the Master approached them. For the first He had words of comfort. For the second He had a smile of tender approval. The third He passed almost abruptly without a word or glance.

The woman said to herself, 'How tenderly the Lord must love this first of His children. The second He was not angry with and yet for her there were no endearments like those given to the first.' She wondered how the third woman had grieved the Lord as He gave her neither look nor passing word.

As in her dream she attempted to account for the action of the Lord, the Master himself confronted her and said:

'Oh, woman of the world, how wrongly you have judged. The first kneeling woman needs all the succour of my constant care to keep her feet in the way. The second has stronger faith and deeper love. But the third, whom I seemed to pass abruptly by, has faith and love of the finest fibre. Her I am preparing by swift processes for the highest and holiest service. She knows, loves and trusts me so perfectly as to be independent of words or looks.'

Jacob now pulls out of Canaan 'with all that he had' and on arrival at Beersheba God speaks to him 'in the visions of the night'. If you do not have such visions do not think it a weakness; Jacob was a stubborn man and needed plenty of them. At Bethel, at Penuel, and now at Beersheba the assuring word comes: 'Fear not to go down into Egypt: for I will there make of you a great nation: I will go down with you into Egypt: and I will also surely bring you up again: and Joseph shall put his hand upon your eyes.' God is so longsuffering and kind and knowing Jacob, and loving him, God meets him at the place of his need. He needed a word from God and he got it.

Change is not easy. Little men with little minds and little imagination go through life in little ruts smugly resisting all changes which would jar their little worlds. Change is not made without inconvenience and the upheaval in the lives of the children of Israel as they took 'their little ones, their wives...their cattle and their goods, which they got in the land of Canaan, and came into Egypt' must have been immense. What they left at that time was to be incalculably rewarded with what the Lord had in the future for them.

So we all have to face change. We pass from school to work, or higher education. We leave home and familiar things for the unfamiliar. In work we sometimes have to change jobs and it is not easy. It means a new home, a new neighbourhood, a new local church. At a later stage we have to retire and move into a new lifestyle. Old landmarks change, friends die, the future seems bleak. Nothing remains the same very long. Even today's software technology is bypassed by better technology tomorrow. Does it frighten you? I'm quite sure that change frightened the patriarch, Jacob, but that changeless voice calmed him down saying, 'I am God, the God of your father.'

Just like Jacob we all need to be reminded of the changeless character of God. Is not the word to the Hebrews of New Testament days one of the greatest promises of all? For me there is no greater word of assurance to any heart than the golden promise of Hebrews 13:8, 'Jesus Christ, the same, yesterday, today and forever'. 'The same' is one of Christ's divine titles. Peter was to discover when his resurrected Saviour stood on the shore and made him his breakfast that neither past behaviour nor present mood had affected the Lord's love for him. It was one of the biggest discoveries of his life. We think the Lord changes just like we do but His ways are not ours. When everything else is obsolete and on the scrap-heap the love, grace, pity and power of the Lord Jesus will remain, exhaustless, indispensable and adaptable to the deepest needs of the human heart. From the days of Jacob and Joseph to the days of Concorde our God has not changed even to the shadow of a turning. We fully appreciate why George Muller, the great man of faith of the last century who had housed 2,000 children in his orphanage, put a framed text in his room. The framed text had two words written on it. They read '... and today'.

So it was that Jacob arrived in Egypt, sending Judah before him to direct his way. 'And Joseph made ready his chariot and went up to meet Israel his father, to Goshen, and presented himself to him: and he fell on his neck and wept on his neck a good while'. There have been few reunions between father and son in history equal to this one. Few men have honoured a parent as Joseph honoured his. Joseph's father was now 130 years of age. He must have been a withered, halting, famine pursued man but it made no difference to the highly sophisticated Joseph. Here was his father, at last, and he wept long on his neck. Joseph was neither ashamed of his father nor of the tears that flowed down his cheeks at the sight of him. Let all young men or women promoted to high positions take note.

When Pharaoh heard of the arrival of Joseph's family he seemed pleased and directed Joseph to care for them but Joseph was not content with that. He brought some of his family to meet the great Pharaoh and finally he brought Jacob. Here was probably the foremost court in the world. There was a great social gulf between Egypt and Canaan, between court and tent, between monarch and shepherd. Joseph was not ashamed to bring the two extremes together. Joseph honoured his father and his days were to be long in the land which the Lord his God had given him.

The interview between Pharaoh and Jacob is fascinating. 'How old are you?', asks the great Egyptian, 'One hundred and thirty!', answers Jacob. 'Few and evil have been the days of my life and they have not attained to the days of the years of the life of my fathers.' What a summary! We cannot help but contrast the tremendous difference between the clear, powerful, God honouring tones of Joseph when he had first been interviewed by Pharaoh and those of his father. It is true that he then 'blessed Pharaoh' and no doubt it was a kindly blessing but somehow Jacob's summary of his life to Pharaoh was more of a moan than a doxology. He raises no theme of exaltation but dismisses his days as few and evil and declares that his forebears had lived longer than he had done. It's true that Terah reached 205 and Abraham 175 and Isaac 180 but could he not have given a better account of himself than only to boast of the longevity of his forebearers? Could he not have praised God for Joseph and related how God had preserved him to the present tremendous hour?

Some men are never happy. It was true that evil had dogged Jacob's steps from boyhood to the death of Rachel and the loss of Joseph but, surely, all his days had not been evil. Was there not something he could have praised God for?

It reminds me of a beautiful autumn day when a friend drove me for a memorable visit to the city of York. We went round all the many historical sites and ambled through the famous 'Shambles' where the beautiful shops belie the name of the district in which they stand.

Suddenly we noticed a shop with a handsomely inscribed text above the door. To our surprise the shop was given over to selling tastefully inscribed Bible texts and cards. We just had to go in. There was an old lady behind the counter and no sooner had we entered the shop than she cheerfully asked, 'Are you believers?' We were delighted to be able to say that we were, whereupon, with a twinkle in her eye, the old lady leaned over the counter and said, 'It's worth a king's ransom to be able to shout Hallelujah!'

That old lady, in her eighties, was right in the tradition of those student zealots of the first Christian Union at Cambridge University who, linking arms, walked down the street in Cambridge singing:

It's better to shout than to doubt,
It's better to rise than to fall,
It's better to let the glory out,
Than to have no glory at all!'

Poor Jacob, what an enigma he was! Let us in whatever situation we find ourselves always be prepared to find something to praise God for. Let's be like old Matthew Henry, the famous Bible commentator, when robbed by a highwayman on a stagecoach journey: 'I'm grateful,' he told friends later. 'Grateful?', asked his friends. 'Yes, grateful it has not happened to me before!'

Yet, no word of criticism passed Joseph's lips. 'And Joseph nourished his father and all his household'. It is interesting to note that Jacob lived until he was 147 so that he enjoyed Joseph's company in Egypt for exactly the same number of years he had spent with him before he was sold into Egypt. God's goodness to Jacob was not only amazing, it was compensatory. God is no man's debtor and if his ways seem strange, time will prove they are always kind.

When Jacob eventually died we read that 'Joseph fell upon his father's face and wept upon him and kissed him'. He then gave him, with Pharaoh's permission, what amounted to a royal funeral. He honoured his father's dying request and had him buried in Canaan. Chariots and horsemen accompanied the cortege to Canaan including all the servants of Pharaoh, the elders of his house, and all the elders of the land of Egypt. 'It was,' comments Scripture, 'a very great gathering'. Yet we cannot help but comment that it was because of Joseph's reputation that Pharaoh so greatly honoured Jacob in his death.

How could anyone sum up Jacob's life? On the one hand he had been genuinely devout and yet on the other he had been utterly self-seeking. He truly loved his mother and his wife and yet he was ever a distrusting and suspicious man. He had high aims but despicable methods. He was a paradox, an enigma. Yet, the Bible constantly refers to 'the God of Jacob'. Why? It is a title of divine mercy and grace. It tells what God's love can do. If He can do such great things for Jacob he can do it for anyone! Despite all his faults, Jacob (meaning 'deceiver') did become Israel (meaning 'a prince with God') and had, as God promised him at Penuel, 'power with God and with men'. However, when all was said and done it must be said that Jacob had to bow to the greatness of his son. Jacob had questioned the feasibility of such a thing ever happening when Joseph had first told of his youthful dream. The years had proved it was more than a dream. Joseph holds then, as now, centre stage.

$\mathscr{W}$AS $\mathscr{J}$OSEPH $\mathscr{A}$ $\mathscr{R}$ACIST?

GENESIS 44: 13-26

JOSEPH HAS HAD HIS CRITICS AND MANY OF THEM HAVE CLUSTERED AROUND HIS ADMINISTRATION OF EGYPT after his family arrived from Canaan. The charge is brought against him that he showed partiality to his own family in providing them with the best of land and bread when everyone else had to pay for their bread and were ordered to move from place to place for the purpose of guaranteeing to them an efficient supply of food as needed. These critics must be answered.

The man who follows a crowd will never be followed by a crowd and Joseph must have found the implementation of his policies in Egypt a very lonely thing. Leadership needs great sensitivity and a very well developed sense of responsibility and Joseph had to influence a nation toward a goal which they would come to find desirable. Joseph's policy was to take steps during the years of plenty in order to economise for the coming years of famine. A tax of one fifth part was made during the seven plenteous years. The food of those good years was stored up against the years of famine. When the famine came the people came to Joseph on Pharaoh's order and bought corn with their money. When their money ran out they bought food with their cattle. When their cattle ran out they offered themselves and their lands for bread. Joseph then bought up the land for Pharaoh and the people entered into the service of Pharaoh.

The children of Israel neither bought corn nor bought land when the crises came. For seven consecutive years the Nile failed to rise. The Egyptologist Brugsch Bey actually discovered heiroglyphic recording such an event dated for the year 1700 B.C. and many accept this as the date for this particular passage of Scripture. The position of the children of Israel seems unfair in comparison to the strictures put upon the Egyptians. The favouritism of Jacob which we have severely criticised in this book now seems to be levelled at his son by some who find his administration racist.

Griffith Thomas has answered the critics very accurately. He points out in his commentary on this passage that it must be remembered that the people of Israel were in Egypt as guests of Pharaoh and there was no possibility of their purchasing food in view of the fact that possessions had all been left behind them. They were distinctly told by Pharaoh not to be anxious about what they possessed in Canaan as the best of Egypt would be theirs (Genesis 45:20). Joseph did nothing which was not clearly sanctioned by Pharaoh, indeed ordered by him and Joseph cannot be blamed for the kindness he showed to his family. Joseph by buying up the land for Pharaoh did not turn the Egyptians into slaves, in fact they were Crown tenants and the tax he imposed was a very moderate one in view of what other countries paid and in view of the great productiveness of the Nile Valley.

The plain fact is that if Joseph had given free corn to the Egyptians it would have resulted in absolute chaos and the black market on corn would have been catastrophic. The wisdom of Joseph during those special years as leader resulted in the salvation of Egypt as well as the providential care of Israel. The Egyptians might have been very jealous of the special attention given to Joseph's family but the fact that Pharaoh owned all the land and all the produce protected them. When a new Pharaoh came who did not know Joseph the very same power was used to try to wipe them out.

Joseph was the key to Israel's salvation all along and his public life was impeccable. His qualities must inspire any person involved in serving the public, especially if they are a believer. Joseph was discreet, he was prompt and thorough in implementing policies and he was always balanced in his reactions to crises that constantly arose in his life. Joseph never returned evil for evil and never sought to take revenge on his enemies. He always saw God's hand in things. Right was might and purity was power. Joseph never excused sin but he was quick to forgive it. He never failed to give God all the glory. His life is a model for all who would serve God in a public way and especially under the full gaze of public scrutiny.

A friend of mine told me of a brilliant medical student in Austria who was an outstanding Christian. He won Austria's highest award in his particular field of study at University and the requirement was that such a student make a speech at the presentation of the award in front of a very distinguished audience including the President of Austria. The young man told his parents that he intended to give the Lord the glory for his achievements and his parents said that if he did so they would walk out and disown him! He made his speech and exalted the Lord Jesus and the entire audience rose and gave a standing ovation! It seems to me that an entire nation gave Joseph the same.

When Joseph's father died there is an incident recorded in Scripture which is a real microcosm of Joseph's secret for living. No sooner had the funeral taken place and the family returned to Egypt than Joseph's brothers said to each other, 'Perhaps Joseph will hate us and may actually repay us for all the evil which we did to him'. It is amazing that after all those years of kindness Joseph's brothers still misunderstood him. They desperately needed reassurance. Approaching Joseph they told him that their father had asked them to ask him for forgiveness, pleading, 'Now please forgive the trespass of the servants of the God of your father'.

Joseph wept when they spoke to him. We cannot be sure whether or not they fabricated the story about their father but when Joseph received their message he again revealed his very sensitive heart.

He wept. It seems to me it was the very same kind of tears as flowed down the Saviour's face when at the grave of Lazarus: the sheer unbelief of man's heart would cause any godly heart to weep. They attributed their own shallow thinking to Joseph but they had not yet learned the true nature of the mind and heart of their brother. He turned to them as they lay prostrate before him and in one sentence revealed the foundation truth in all his theology. Always seek to know a person's theology for it will tell you about their behaviour.

'Am I in the place of God?' he said, 'But as for you, you meant evil against me; but God meant it for good, in order to bring it about as it is today.' Joseph clearly believed that although everything that happened to him was not necessarily good it clearly would work together for good. Joseph acknowledged that they had done wrong and that was good for them to hear but Joseph also showed that he believed that God was using all the experiences of his life to accomplish Divine purposes.

Show me a man, woman or child who lived with such a belief and I will show you that such a belief adds great contentment to their lives. Every difficulty will be an opportunity to them instead of every opportunity being a difficulty. They will learn that nothing happens by chance. What we think is all wrong in the circumstances of our lives God is actually turning around for our good. If Joseph left any legacy of theology during those special years as leader of Egypt his theology of the sovereignty of God in life and lip must stand foremost.

I never tire of repeating the story of Amy Carmichael who lived as a child at Millisle in Co. Down. Amy tells the story in the form of a poem.

'Just a lovely child,
Three years old,
And a mother with a heart
All of gold,
Often did that mother say,

Jesus hears us when we pray,
For He's never far away,
And He always answers.

Now that tiny little child,
Had brown eyes,
And she wanted blue instead,
Like blue skies,
For her mother's eyes were blue,
Like forget-me-nots. She knew
All her mother said was true,
Jesus always answered.

So she prayed for two blue eyes,
Said 'Goodnight',
Went to sleep in deep content,
And delight.
Woke up early, climbed a chair,
By a mirror. Where, O where
Could the blue eyes be? not there;
Jesus hadn't answered.

Hadn't answered her at all;
Never more
Could she pray: her eyes were brown
As before.
Did a little soft wind blow?
Came a whisper soft and low,
'Jesus answered. He said 'No';
Isn't 'No' an answer?'

Many years later when Amy founded the famous Dohnavur
Fellowship in India to save many children from being sold to Hindu
parents for evil practices a visitor asked one of the Indian children
why she thought Indian children seemed to love Amy Carmichael

so much. 'That's easy', said the child, 'she's got the same colour of eyes as we have!'

Whether it is the problem of being thrown in a pit or having what appears to be the wrong colour of eyes it all works together for good to those who love God and to those who are the called according to His purpose. Joseph was no racist, neither was he a bigot, his faith in God reached out, as the Psalmist commented, 'Over the wall' and millions were grateful. Egyptian and Israelite were to rise up and call him blessed. Would to God we had more like him today.

'There aren't just enough songs about Heaven.'

JONI EARICKSON TADA

THE BEST IS KEPT TO THE LAST

GENESIS 50: 22-26

I HAVE THIS FRIEND WHO ONCE SAID HE WANTED ME TO PREACH AT HIS FUNERAL SERVICE. YOU PROBABLY HAVE a mental picture of a very morbid individual who lives with pessimism as his chief motivation, but, you would be wrong. 'I want you to preach on Joseph's bones', he said. What was he on about? Let's investigate.

'And Joseph said to his brethren, "I am dying; but God will surely visit you and bring you out of this land of which he swore to Abraham, to Isaac and to Jacob". Then Joseph took an oath from the children of Israel saying, "God will surely visit you and you shall carry up my bones from hence." So, Joseph died, being one hundred and ten years old: and they embalmed him, and he was put in a coffin in Egypt.'

It is quite obvious from his last words that Joseph was not afraid to die. The very same hope in God which had inspired him all his life was just as real when facing the last enemy. When dying, Joseph's thoughts were not engrossed by his own concerns but rather he was concerned to comfort the hearts of those he left behind.

'What are you crying for? My wife is in Heaven,' said a Christian doctor who had just been bereaved. 'We are not weeping for her,' replied a woman, 'we are weeping for you, doctor.' In his final words he let them all know that although they were losing him, their great benefactor, they had a far better friend in Heaven who would visit them and bring them again out of Egypt.

The implication of Joseph's words was that the people of God would have to pass through a time when God would seem to stand at a distance from them. He foresaw that after his death things would turn unpleasant. Oppression would come but they must not forget the promise of God to Abraham, Isaac and Jacob. Every Israelite in Egypt considered himself a stranger in it and looked forward with deep longing to the time of entering into the land of promise. The promise of God was Joseph's great hope when he was dying. They must not bury his bones in Egypt they must take his bones and bury them in Canaan when, at last, God would take them there. Note that Joseph did not ask to be buried in Canaan immediately after his death like his father had been. He probably knew Pharaoh might not easily give permission for this as he had for his father. The Egyptians were jealous for their great hero, Joseph. Anyhow, the Israelites might have used it as an excuse to get out of Egypt before it was God's time to move. Joseph's last words were not only full of hope for a coming day but they showed great wisdom and timing. The best was kept to the last. The oath they took promising to bury him in Canaan would for two hundred years turn Israelitish minds toward Canaan. That they believed Joseph's prophecy was proved by the fact that they embalmed his body. Embalming preserved the body from putrefaction. Joseph was not buried in Egypt but his body was put in a coffin to await the incredible day when God would visit his people as Joseph had predicted.

The intervention came in the most undramatic way. God's moves are so often unobtusive. He feeds the birds of the forest or spreads your breakfast table and there is not a word of Him. He sends the dew upon the earth or guides the stars upon their way and He doesn't even leave a footprint! When He came to free Israel from Egyptian bondage it took the dramatic plagues and the fearful might of the avenging angel before Pharaoh eventually let Israel go but we must always remember that it was an infant's tears which brought freedom for a nation. Baby Moses had cried in the ark of bullrushes and his tears touched Pharaoh's daughter and the door opened that eventually led to God taking Israel to Canaan. On small hinges do the mighty doors of destiny swing.

When the great exodus of the Hebrew people took place, Moses ordered that Joseph's bones be brought with them. Right through the wilderness journey those bones were kept almost as a treasure! At last the day came and Joseph's dying wish was carried out. He was buried at Shechem in the land of Canaan not far from the spot where his brothers had plotted against his life and cast him into a pit. Few funeral services have been more packed with meaning for the living.

So, the friend who asked me to preach on Joseph's bones was not being morbid after all! Here is a message of hope and faith which reaches down to us today. Think of all the personal qualities of Joseph. He was guileless, tactful, sensitive, balanced, courageous, wise, humble, resolute, considerate, sympathetic, patient, family orientated but at the same time exercising great executive power. He was holy but was 'no pain-in-the-neck' with it. He was unquestionably, intellectually brilliant but he was also filled with God's Spirit. He feared God and he hated sin. He referred everything to God as if it were as natural as breathing, but, it was that final action that crowns his life. 'By faith,' is Joseph's New Testament epitaph, 'When he was dying, made mention of the departure of the children of Israel and gave instructions concerning his bones.' (Hebrews 11:22). The best was kept to the last.

The Christian lives in a world very different to Joseph's. Christians face the dying culture of the latter part of the 20th century. They face the breakdown of morality and the rise of false cults. International terrorism is rampant in virtually every nation. What can the Christian do? As Joseph looked to an earthly Canaan, we look to a Heavenly.

Joseph looked beyond his present plight of imminent death to the promises of God for the future. So must we. God will surely visit us for 'The Lord himself shall descend from Heaven with a shout, with the voice of the archangel, and with the trump of God: and the dead in Christ shall rise first: Then we who are alive and remain shall be caught up together with them in the clouds, to meet the Lord in the air: and so shall we ever be with the Lord' (1 Thessalonians 4: 16-17).

Millions of Christians speak of Heaven and wonder what it will bring. C. S. Lewis said: 'Joy is the serious business of Heaven'. Joni Earickson Tada sings that 'There just aren't enough songs about Heaven'. Dr. Martyn Lloyd-Jones was dying and his daughter, Lady Catherwood and her sister were praying by the great Bible teacher's bedside. They prayed that the Lord would spare their father just a little while longer. The man of God leaned over and wrote a note to his daughter and in great physical weakness handed it to her. It read, 'Don't hinder me from the glory!' What a way to die! What a Joseph-like action.

A. W. Pink said, 'One breath of paradise will extinguish all the adverse winds of earth'. Richard Baxter said, 'There is nothing but Heaven worth setting our minds upon'. Vance Havner said, 'A dog is at home in this world because this is the only one a dog will ever live in. We are not at home in this world because we are made for a better one'. R. M. McCheyne said, 'If it be sweet to be the growing corn of the Lord here, how much better to be gathered into His barn'. Matthew Henry said, 'Our duty is always to keep Heaven in our eye and earth under our feet'.

The questions that flood our minds, though. Is Heaven a real place? Where is it? If I am a Christian would I go to Heaven immediately? How long would it take me to get there? Would I know my friends? Would they know me? What would I look like in Heaven? Would I have the same body? Could I eat? For millions, Heaven is a great mystery but the Bible has not left us in the dark about it. Let's see what the Scriptures say about it.

Is Heaven a real place! Yes, John 14:2 and 3 quotes our Lord as saying, 'I go to prepare a place for you'. Matthew 6 teaches that we are to lay up for ourselves treasures in Heaven. So, it is not a state of mind. What kind of place is it? It is a place of indescribable beauty and glory. 'Eye has not seen nor ear heard, nor has it entered into the heart of man, the things which God has prepared for those who love him, but God has revealed them to us through his Spirit,' says 1 Corinthians 2:9. As we read the Word of God the Spirit of God can fill our hearts with a very real and heartening revelation of what is to come.

Heaven is a place of perfect rest. 'Blessed are the dead who die in the Lord from now on', says Revelation 14:13, 'Yes,' says the Spirit, 'that they may rest from their labours and their works follow them'. People on earth never really know what it means to rest. Why, the very cow in the field lies down to chew the cud after a meal but humans are up from their meals and rushing on to do a dozen other things. We cannot even stop to enjoy the beauty of the earth around us. As Robert Frost put it:

'The woods are lovely, dark and deep,
But I have promises to keep,
And miles to go before I sleep.'

Heaven is a place of open vision. The things that happen down here are so hard to understand, unemployment, heartache, illness, disappointment, sorrow. It is not easy to see that all things work together for good to them that love God. One thing is for sure. You may not be able to trace God in everything in your life but you can always trust Him. He sometimes seems to draw straight lines with what appears to be a crooked stick. We cannot explain everything now. We cannot see as God sees. But in Heaven we will know. Heaven is a place of open vision with no glass between. There we will understand as we cannot understand now what has been happening in the circumstances of our lives. 'Now we see through a glass darkly; but then face to face; now I know in part but then shall I know even as I am known', says Paul.

A little boy was in the habit of gazing in at the toy soldiers through the window of the local toyshop. The owner of the shop got used to the child constantly looking in his window and when he had missed him from his accustomed habit for a few days he enquired if all was well with the lad. He discovered that the boy had had an accident and was unconscious in a local hospital. The toyshop owner asked permission of the child's mother to take the toy soldiers to the lad as a gift. He got to the hospital and quietly left the box of soldiers by the lad's bedside. When the boy came out of unconsciousness one of the very first things he saw was the box of soldiers and with disbelief he grabbed the box and exuberantly said to his mother, 'Oh, look, mother! Look! Here are the soldiers and there is no glass between'.

Peter uses negatives when describing Heaven because there is nothing here to fully describe what is there. 'An inheritance incorruptible and undefiled, and that does not fade away, reserved in Heaven for you'. If the symbolism of Heaven used in Scripture is so fabulous what will the reality be like! Even if we were to find a word, phrase or sentence to describe Heaven we would not, it would almost seem, be permitted to disclose it! This was Paul's problem when he wrote of the man he knew 'Fourteen years ago, whether in the body I do not know, or whether out of the body I do not know, God knows, how he was caught up into Paradise and heard inexpressible words, which it is not lawful for a man to utter'. Perhaps it was because of that vision that Paul was never able to settle for earth. He writes to the Philippians that he has a desire to depart to be with Christ which is far better. He tells the Corinthians that he would prefer to be away from the body and at home with the Lord.

We find it very hard to believe that despite all the frustrations, difficulties and the problems of life, death for the Christian is actually better than life and that to die is gain. That does not give us the right to believe in euthanasia nor suicide. The Lord gives life and the Lord takes it away. Death transports the Christian to gain. As Canaan was Joseph's goal and the goal of the pilgrimage of the people of God in the Old Testament so Heaven is the land of our desire, the land of our promise. It is actually called, in the book of Hebrews, 'A Sabbath rest' for the people of God. We have various ideas about the Sabbath, but in Scripture it has the idea of fulfilment, completion. God rested on the Sabbath. It was a source of endless delight for Him, of endless exploration. That's what Heaven will be for us. It will be 'A Sabbath rest' when we can explore the richness and fullness of all that God is in Christ. It will be unutterable and inexhaustible love.

'Oh the deep, deep love of Jesus,
'Twould take ages to explore,
Just one drop of that vast ocean,
Just one grain from off its shore'

Heaven will mean the glory of revelation and the revelation of glory. Jesus said, 'Father, I desire that they also whom you gave me may be with me where I am, that they may behold my glory'.

The question is asked will the saved go to Heaven immediately? The answer is a definite yes for to be absent from the body is to be present with the Lord. In fact there are only two places a Christian can ever be: in the body or with the Lord. The body is only the house in which the Christian lives; when death comes the soul will leave the body and go immediately to be with Christ. The question is also raised as to whether we will know one another in Heaven. The answer is also a definite yes. Jesus said, 'When you see Abraham, Isaac and Jacob and all the prophets in the Kingdom of God'. Moses and Elijah knew each other on the Mount of Transfiguration and they still had the same names. They knew each other though they had never met on earth. 'Then', Paul says in 1 Corinthians 13:12 'shall I know even as also I am known.'

Just as Joseph's words brought hope to the beleaguered Children of Israel, so the sacred promises of God's Word of the coming prospect of Heaven with its revel and rule brings incalculable encouragement and hope to the Christian under stress and strain, disappointment and trial.

As sure as Joseph's word was true so the Saviour's word to those He loved before He departed is also true: 'I will come again and receive you unto myself that where I am there you may be also'. The thought cheers the hardest day.

So we must take our leave of the fascinating Joseph. I pray that what I said in the preface of this little book has proved to be true. I pray that you have been captivated by the loveliness of the character and behaviour of the son of Jacob and Rachel. One wonders what his entrance into Heaven must have been like. 'Good and faithful servant' must have been his Divine commendation but, somehow, for millions of us who await the second coming of our wonderful Lord, Joseph still stands near us, pointing upward.

The believer does not choose where he or she will serve the Lord. That is the Lord's choice. Joseph wanted Canaan but he got Egypt. You may want to serve the Lord in India but He may want you to serve Him in Cullybackey. You may want to stay and teach in your tiny Sunday school class in Pucket's Creek or in Tillicoultry but God may want you to teach His Word to thousands across the world. Joseph's life has proved that what God wants is best. Let us leave the choice with Him. The simplest life can relay blessings which can move a continent for God. Thank you for reading this short life of Joseph and may God use you all the days of your life. You can be one of God's men or women for your generation. My advice to you is: don't just dream it – be it!

Derick Bingham

RUTH

*R*uth, whose name in Hebrew means 'Beautiful', did not seem to have success on her side. There had been three deaths in her household, she was poverty stricken and had to begin a new life, in a new land, gleaning alien corn. Yet, this unknown Moabitess through marriage became one of the most outstanding women in the world's history, in literature, and in God's eternal plan.

Through her Royal Household was born the Saviour of the world. In this book the author traces her amazing story and tries to draw a few lessons for people, everywhere.

CONTENTS

$\mathscr{I}$NTRODUCTION

SUDDENLY, IN THE MIDST OF A BUSY DAY A LETTER DROPS ONTO YOUR DOORMAT. IT PROVES TO BE A LOVE letter. It is private. It says things to you that transcends the hectic traffic outside. You are transported out of the mundane nitty-gritty everyday routine by a warm, loving, inspiring feeling. You have received more than a letter: You have been delivered a message to your heart which has made your day and the rest of your life, perhaps, different.

The message from Ruth in the Bible is like that. It lies between the warring, murdering, scheming stories of the Book of Judges and often frightening turbulent days which are recorded in the two books of Samuel. It is a love story. Yet it is more than just a story of a romance between a desperately poor girl and a very wealthy land owner: it is a story of love for God, of love for His people and all that they believe.

I wrote this little book just after the death of my mother. I wrote it in just one week staying quietly by the sea at Clifden in Connemara, at the Abbeyglen Hotel near where Alcock and Brown landed after the first epic transatlantic flight from America to the continent of Europe. I was 22 and was extremely naive and inexperienced in many areas of life but the comfort and calm, inspiration and guidance I received in my young heart from this biblical love story was an experience I will never forget.

The story begins with a tragedy, but then out of the womb of all tragedy there comes something beautiful, which if the tragedy had never occurred, would never have been seen. Great pleasure has been experienced by countless millions of people as a result of the lessons learned from the pain of Ruth's story. Facing tragedy, loneliness and poverty Ruth allowed God to have His way in her life and accepted the rough with the smooth as the matchless Divine Potter slowly moulded her into the person He wanted her to be. Come, let us walk together through those long ago days in Israel, as John Keats would have put it, 'Amidst alien corn'. The message of Ruth is ultimately very simple: God always goes where He is wanted.

Derick Bingham
Belfast 1992

'TILL LONELINESS AND DEATH STEP UP TO GREET ME

'Duties are ours, events are the Lord's'
SAMUEL RUTHERFORD

LONELINESS HURTS AND IT CAN COME IN THE STRANGEST PLACES. I CAN THINK OF TWO PLACES IT hurt me.

It was a beautiful hot August afternoon and we were in New York City to preach about the Lord Jesus. Having no engagements that afternoon I took myself to the centre of the city and walked the length of Fifth Avenue from West Fifty-seventh Street corner to Times Square and back. Thousands upon thousands of people were on the street, laughing, talking and jostling. Young girls with their leather shoulder bags swinging along; smooth American businessmen with great knotted neck ties; small suntanned children charging here, there and yonder. Saks, Tiffanys, and all the rest were drawing their customers. I had dreamed of this place, but as I stood watching it all I felt about as lonely as if I were on the top of Slieve Donard in Ulster with the wind tugging my coat. Alone in a strange land!

Strange things may fascinate, but when you are alone in facing them: loneliness can sting. You know what I mean. You are taken into a crowded room and are introduced to the 'in' set. They smile at you, say the right thing and then turn to each other and go right on where they left off. In the end you busy yourself reading the words on a record sleeve or something just as irrelevant in order to cover the loneliness you feel. You have not got the right school tie on or don't drive the proper make of car; so you don't make it.

There is a beautiful little phrase used by the ever-gentle Amy Carmichael which sums up the answer to loneliness in a strange land. Talking of India and the most complicated work of trying to save girls from child prostitution and the snake of the subsequent evils she wrote:

> 'It was in gentle, generous, patient ways like this that we learned not to fear any strange land. Even if He is the only one whom we know there, He is enough'.

He is enough? We were far away from Fifth Avenue as the train rocketed on into the night. Five of us, all college students, were in our bunks on the edge of dream.

I could hear the boys breathing heavily and dropping off to sleep one by one, for me it simply would not come. I tried them all counting sheep, jumping a gate, telling my toes to settle and relax, then my legs, then my whole body. It was useless because my sheep got stuck in the bars of the gate and nearly broke their necks, and my toes were in an unsettled mood.

I threw back the small curtain of the train window and gazed out as the small Russian villages seemingly swam past. A thousand miles from home, in a very strange land, coupled with an ominous feeling regarding the Communist regime that surrounded me did not make me feel uplifted. Alone in a strange land!

The Bible lay on the bunk and reaching over I opened it. The ancient words stared up at me and thrilled my very soul: 'My peace I give unto you, not as the world giveth give I unto you ... Let not your heart be troubled, neither let it be afraid'. I had Him, and He was enough. I was asleep in two minutes.

Ruth, the Moabitess was lonely because of death. Widowhood for this beautiful girl had come early in life and, believe me, it was as real to her as to a Jacqueline Kennedy or a Coretta King. Death to most people, until it comes to their own door, is distant. People are sorry, yes, but do not remain sorrowful. Tears do not seem to flow when death is down the road. Let it take a mother, a father, a brother or a sister from your house and you'll know all about the empty room, the missing voice, the vacuum that will never again be filled. You never get over missing them: you just have to get used to living without them. It was no different three thousand years ago.

But not only one death had come to Ruth's door. There were two more. Chilion, her husband, Mahlon, her brother-in-law, and Elimelech, her father-in-law. Three males out of one house is a strange occurrence. The details are not given as to the causes of death, but it would seem that the death of Ruth's husband in particular had come early in her married life because there is no record of any children. Then, to add to it all, there was a famine in the land. In Ireland we know only too well what that can mean. The very place in which these words are being written on the Connemara coast was ravaged by famine a few decades ago and thousands perished. The old folk can tell you stories to this day. Hunger, death and loneliness all stepping up to greet you does not exactly make a success story.

That, of course, is the very kind of situation in which God works. With us there is a difficulty in every opportunity, but with Him there is an opportunity in every difficulty. Watch now, as God begins to work in the storm tossed life of the Moabitess lass. There are lessons to be learned here which if you can learn now, will save you countless heartbreaks later.

In the Bible story of Ruth over fifty out of a total of eighty-five verses are taken up with dialogue, so it is obvious that the writer (probably Samuel) prefers to tell his story through conversations. The first series of conversations occurring after the tragedy and at the time of famine are primarily taken up with reaction to the situation. Reaction to situations has a bigger part to play in life than we can ever imagine. Your reaction to trouble, when it comes, steers the ship of life through the storm to the harbour or onto the rocks. Watch as God records their reactions. Her mother-in-law's reaction comes first, her sister-in-law's second, and Ruth's third.

Naomi, the Bible indicates, was the first to move. 'Then she arose with her daughters-in-law that she might return from the country of Moab; for she had heard in the country of Moab how that the Lord had visited His people in giving them bread'. That she should not have moved away in the first place, most theologians are agreed. Elimelech, her husband, had maybe more to do with it than she. Her name means 'Pleasure' but when she eventually got home to Bethlehem she said, 'Call me not Naomi, call me Mara ... (bitterness) ... I went out full, and the Lord hath brought me home again empty'. She was, like many another, far away from the Lord. Like you, maybe. Once close, happy, nothing between you and the Saviour you had trusted. Your Bible was your delight, Christian fellowship was your companionship, prayer was your very spiritual breath. Now you are cold, critical, and miserable. Spiritual things you keep up outwardly, mechanically even, to make a show because you have an old reputation to keep. Your heart is far from Him. You did not even bend your knees today to the One who thought it worthwhile to shed His blood for you at Calvary. You are neither happy 'in the world' or 'in the church'. You are neither hot nor cold. Don't worry, I've been there many times. As dead as the letter of the law. All talk and no power. All truth and no burning love for the Lord Jesus. Famine in your soul, filled with loneliness in that you no longer have His close companionship, and experiencing spiritual death in your effectiveness for God.

But 'she arose'. She knew what was wrong. She knew where the answer lay. God had not run away, she had. She 'went out full'; have you? Money and affluence have deadened your zeal. Things matter more than God. Maybe the Lord is bringing you back empty to give you Himself again. It reminds me of my friend, James Barton. He told me how he was sickened by the material grabbing Christians in the West. He has given his life to working for the spreading of the Gospel in India and he told me of how much the spirit of materialism hurt his soul. At his gate, opening onto a street, there lives a family. They actually live on the street. The little boys go to school from there and return there at night. No roof over their heads, just a little corner at Jimmy's gate. Can you imagine my friend's reaction when his own little boy asked his dad could he give his worn-out jeans to his little friend at the gate? Shame on us and our grumblings. Maybe it would be good for us to be stripped to find that His grace is sufficient for us. Arise and go back to Him now. Go to your knees this very moment. The Lord has not moved away. His love is absolutely unchanging. He loves you still.

Orpah, which means 'stiff-necked' comes next. Her reaction was understandable, but came so near the pathway of success that it is one of the saddest points in the story. Her husband was gone; her father-in-law had died and now she accompanies Naomi to the border of His land. She is counselled by Naomi to return to 'her people' and 'her gods'. Let us not be too quick to blame Orpah. Obedience is not a virtue either to be overlooked or censured. She kissed her mother-in-law and returned to Moab.

'To kiss' and 'to cling' nevertheless, are two very different reactions. They both speak volumes. Proximity does not mean affinity, and a kiss can even be casual. The words 'but Ruth clung to her' made all the difference in the world. Ruth could not go; her woman-heart clung on. She did not kiss: she clung ! She tells Naomi of her great pledge. She wants to go where she goes, live where she lives. Naomi's people are to become her people and most important of all, Naomi's God is to be hers. She even wants to lie in the same grave.

If you and I had happened, by chance, to come walking past these two women we would probably have walked on. Just two women talking by the side of the road; the wind blowing up dust as usual, the sun pouring down on the quiet countryside at the time of barley harvest.

Yet, things are never as they seem. In the heart of that beautiful girl there struggled the biggest decision in her young life. She had discovered the true God and was she going to go back to the worldly substitutes in Moab that never satisfy? The loneliness of an alien land, the future seemingly blank, with little chance of gaining a husband, or the ease of familiar things? It's the old and endless question. God calls, we hear and ... ?

It came to a young sophisticated prince in the courts of Pharaoh; an alien wilderness with a load of grumblers or his social whirl ? What was it to be? It was a lonely decision and very few people noticed when he made it even those who were supposed to be on his side were against him. Did he lose? Forty-six years later, with the Red Sea, through which he led over a million people, the wilderness, and all the many miracles behind him, God takes a body and buries it on Mount Nebo. The body ? That of the greatest leader of men history has ever seen. The meekest man in all the earth. He did not look it when he walked out of the palace that day.

Abram was called out to an alien land. He probably looked rather naive that day when he headed out of Ur of the Chaldees. He never dreamt that he was to father a great nation which Hitler's third Reich, Egypt's Nasser, *or* Russia herself could not break. But he believed God and it was accounted unto him for righteousness. He staggered not.

Miserable teenager! Scruff! Idiot! Running down a valley with a stone on a sling against a man with a spear the size of a telegraph pole; never talk about his size. 'What are you doing, David? He will give your flesh for the birds to eat.' 'The Lord of Hosts, I believe in Him.' 'Yes, so do I, but aren't you a little bold for your age? I mean, why draw the criticism of older and wiser men than you?' 'The giant has defied the Lord and sitting around talking or arguing about the best way to bring him down won't do him any harm. I'm going to do something about it; let me go at him in the name of the Lord of Hosts.'

The teenager made the decision himself and as far as I can see there was not a single man in all Israel who agreed with him, good, godly and right though they may have been; except the Lord. THAT made all the difference and lo, the giant came tumbling down.

He looked stupid at the time but he became king afterwards.

It is always so! A young man here, a girl there, gets directions from the Lord for their life's work. Nobody pats them on the back, or rings them up on the phone to congratulate them when they decide to follow it. No Nobel prize comes their way. 'Israel' sits back and watches how they will fare. If they are blessed, that is good; if they fail, we knew they would anyway.

The Lord, however, still lives in His heaven and His ways are not the ways of men. He noticed the heart of the girl and her decision as she stood on the road that day. He knew she was seeking His comfort and guidance. Nobody who ever reached out for that comfort and guidance was ever disappointed. It is the set of the sails and not the gales that tell us the way to go. Ruth's sails were set.

> *Who packed thy wallet, friend?*
> *One whose love shall never end -*
> *What therein was laid?*
> *He put in bread and wine and stayed.*
> *What said He thereon?*
> *'Wilt thou want more than these*
> *when thou art gone?'*
> *How didst thou answer Him?*
> *I begged a candle, for mine eyes were dim.*
> *He bent on me His gaze*
> *Clearer than a thousand days,*
> *'Thou shalt need no light*
> *by any day or night.'*
> *Then said I, 'My fear*
> *Was of a blackness when no hand was near.'*
> *But He this word let fall:*
> *'I shall not leave thee when thou leavest all.'*
> *And wilt thou take a staff?*
> *Of His cross He gave me half.*
> *What shall be thy dress?*

He clothed me in emptiness.
Dost thou need no book?
His face is all whereon I crave to look.
Hast thou no map or chart?
I know my road, it leadeth to His heart.

AMIDST ALIEN CORN

'Give me the love that leads the way,
The faith that nothing can dismay,
The hope no disappointment hire,
The passion that will burn like fire.
Let me not sink to be a clod -
Make me Thy fuel, flame of God.'

SO, OUT OF THE BLUE THERE COMES SHOWERS OF BLESSING - RUTH FINDS WEALTH, HAPPINESS, AND HER man? Not so fast. God is never in any hurry. To find and do God's will is not accomplished all in the one day. He spent forty years training Moses after he yielded to His will. David fought a lion and a bear before he faced Goliath. Amos was first a shepherd in Tekoa. John lived in the wilderness. Peter had to learn his own weaknesses in the judgment hall before he led three thousand to his Lord at Pentecost. Paul first went to Arabia before he went to Jerusalem.

When you are under God's training the hardest lesson of all is to wait for Him. Work for Him, pray to Him, read about Him but, to wait for Him, there is the rub.

'They that wait upon the Lord shall renew their strength. They shall reap and not faint.'

To find the will of God for one's life is probably the most difficult task in Christian existence. To search for it is not to degenerate into the merely interesting, the pretty. There is blood and iron in it. How am I to know? To the right or to the left? This job or that? Can I know, now? I always wanted to. To know, now; a voice out of the sky whispering, 'go here, now there'. But it just doesn't work that way.

The greatest guiding line to follow when faced with a decision as a Christian, I have found, is to shut your door. Get the influences of life out of the way and explain everything in secret to your heavenly Father. Acknowledge Him. Then go and act in a common sense manner according to your abilities and limitations. When you acknowledge Him He then directs your paths. Ask two simple questions, 'Is it right?' and, 'Is it necessary?' If there is no cloud between you and your Lord, go ahead. There is a word they use in the Far East for the phrase Paul wrote when he explained God's will as 'Good ... acceptable ... and perfect'. They say it should be that 'Good and perfect and lovable will of God'. If you submit, acknowledge and then act, you will find it will become not always pleasurable, but eventually lovable.

Such was the case with my heroine, Ruth. It was right and necessary that she should look after Naomi. She acknowledged the Lord in all her ways. God acted. He was, by promise, bound to. It is just like my Irish friend, David, who was almost killed in a terrorist bomb explosion. The bomb had injured him in the face and weeks after that deadly hour I was overhauling the universe with him around a blazing fire. What was his reaction to the whole thing? Quietly looking at me he said: 'If God can bring order out of the chaos of the cross, He can bring order out of the chaos of my face.' Those words are alive in me even now.

She went, and gleaned in the field after the reapers and 'her hap was' to light on a part of the field belonging unto Boaz, who was of the kindred of Elimelech. It was a singular field. The system used in the Bethlehem - Judah of those days was different to our idea of farming. We imagine farmers with individual fields owned by the farmer, but this was not the case. There appears to be a common field where all grow their crops, with ownership vested in parts of the one great field. Not hedges but stones separated the various sections.

There is enough in that phrase 'Her hap was' to keep me writing until the end of this book. Apparently, by chance, Ruth came to glean corn in a section of the field belonging to a mighty man of wealth called Boaz. The phrase 'Her hap was' shows clearly that she did not understand the full significance of what she was doing.

There is the secret. She had acknowledged the Lord, and it was no happening that she walked into Boaz's section, though at the time she thought nothing of it.

Just like Philip. Do you think it was a happening that Philip many centuries later ran and joined himself to a chariot owned by an Ethiopian Government Cabinet Member at the very moment the official was reading a verse about the Lord Jesus that needed explaining? God told Philip to run and if he had not, he would have arrived at the wrong verse. A happening?

How much of our life resembles
Time lost in going upstairs;
What days and weeks seem wasted,
But we're climbing unawares.

The simple fact is that in ten years time you may look back and find that the most important thing you did this year was to open a door, walk across a street or bump into a friend. Little things have fascinating repercussions. A word here, a word there, can ripple through eternity. Watch the little things. It so happened that a man who cared for young people went into a store in Boston and spoke of the Lord Jesus to a young 'shoe shop' assistant. Nobody knew that conversation would result in Dwight L. Moody, the young assistant, moving, under God, thousands upon thousands to find the same Lord Jesus. One was C. T. Studd who in turn led thousands in Africa to the Saviour. Another was a lady in Co. Antrim, Ulster, whose son I was preaching with the other night, and he is over sixty years of age!

We could go on! We were standing in the office of Jim Vaus not long ago. His room was filled with huge computers and he was explaining to some doctors about a system he was developing to aid them in administrative work.

As he talked we sat at the back of the room and our minds wandered back to nineteen forty-six when Jim was a notorious criminal with one million dollars to his name accumulated by devious means. His brilliant knowledge of electronics had been used in entirely the wrong direction.

He sat that night listening to a young preacher called Billy Graham as he told of the story of a Saviour's love and how if repenting of sin, a person could find forgiveness and salvation, by accepting the Saviour's death as sufficient in God's eyes to cover all his sins. Jim did just that! The result? As we winged our way home, out of New York, in Jim's little four-seater plane I asked Vaus's pilot-assistant what he thought of his boss. A self-confessed non-Christian, he said: 'When Vaus came into this place there were one hundred and forty youth gangs in this area and now there are none!'

Remember this all started when the young Christian whose preaching was used of God to win Jim to saving faith in the nineteen-forties got down on his knees and handed himself over completely to his Master for the preaching of the Gospel. I know, because he told me so himself! Little things. I have come to believe that in life it is the little things that are big and important and the seemingly big things small, empty, boring, and in the end very insignificant. It is like the correspondence between Victor Hugo and his publisher Hurst and Blackell in 1862.

The author was on holiday and anxious to know how his new novel 'Les Miserables' was selling. He wrote: '?' The reply was: '!' Little things mean much more than they appear. Watch them as for your very life.

Hard, backbreaking work it was, gleaning. Her very presence there showed that she was in the poverty bracket. Yet, God, ever gracious, had provided for the widows. It was laid down in His law that at harvest time a man must not reap his land to the very border, nor should he pick up what was left after the reapers went through. If he forgot a sheaf and left it in the field he was forbidden to go back for it. That was for the gleaner. I wonder sometimes just what thoughts were Ruth's as she gleaned in the heavy sun. This surely was the path of poverty and brokenness.

Is it any different for those of us who are sick and tired of the standard average life of the Christian world around us?

A life of ease and talk, of looking over the shoulder at each other before we move for God?

Tired of the emptiness of our prayer lives and our own preaching that lacks the sweet, direct, recognisable touch of the Holy Spirit? Those of us, and those would include every man and child who knows and loves the Lord Jesus, who are longing for a mighty revival to be poured out upon our land before the Master returns: and we wait and wait and wait. Wherein lies our weakness?

It lies in our lack of brokenness before God. We must rise from our ease to our knees and tell the Lord that without Him we can do nothing, nothing, NOTHING! It will mean losing the smile of the sophisticated circle; it will mean sacrifice and time alone at His sorely wounded feet. It is not the popular thing ... it is the only thing.

What do I mean? I mean just this, Let me illustrate: We had been given a direction from God one day to hold an Open Air Service in an Irish country 'grazing field' to proclaim the Gospel. It was something which some thought foolish. 'We are in a modern society, moon walking and all that ... modern men do not go to grazing fields to hear the Gospel.' Despite the critics we called a day of prayer. There they were - twenty men on their knees for hours. Suddenly as somebody was praying, the tears started pouring down his face. A strange stillness came into the room. Now everybody was sobbing. This was no worked up emotionalism ... the man who was praying was praying for his wayward daughter who was without the Saviour. Never in all of my life did I sit in a prayer meeting like it. The power from then on was indescribable. When we rose the next day to preach the Gospel in the field to the hundreds gathered, it was no surprise to see them there. Nor was it a surprise in the darkness of the night when an eighteen-year-old came to see us so burdened that she must find Christ as her Saviour before the day ended. She did and she was not the only one.

'Have I been so long with thee,
And yet hast thou not known Me ?
0 my Master, I have found Thee
On the roads of Galilee.'

'Have I been so long time with thee
On the roads of Galilee,
Yet, My child, thou hast not known Me
Walking on the tossing sea?'

'O my Master, I have known Thee
On the roads and on the sea.'
'Wherefore then hast thou not known Me
Broken in Gethsemane?'

'I would have thee follow, know Me
Thorn-crowned, nailed upon the tree.
Can'st thou follow, wilt thou know Me,
All the way to Calvary?'

The weekend passed and on the Monday night we went to the place of preaching again. At that time it was my privilege to preach with a young local head master, Robert Hewitt. Words to describe people are sometimes meaningless and hard to choose, but suffice is to say that there are few in Ireland like him. Humble, dedicated, down-to-earth with a reserved spirit that adds a touch of gentleness to all that he does. He loves the Lord Jesus dearly. He rose to speak after I was through and suddenly something happened. The tears started to pour down his cheeks. Robert crying!! I had never seen him crying before in my life and I have seen him in some places where anyone would have broken. He was talking about the cross. A power gripped that congregation so much so that my friend, broken under the power of the message, could not go on. He simply sat down and sobbed his heart out. A cultured, college trained, well respected headmaster breaking his heart when describing the sufferings of his Saviour. There, there, there is the secret of power - brokenness! No advertising, no organisation, no oratory, no 'plastic' evangelism could do that. Send more and more of it to this island, Lord! Break us! Melt us! Humble us! Be glorified! I could not close the meeting. The whole place was so obviously under the power of the Spirit. I had only heard one man describe such a happening as I was witnessing now. A gentle, humble, Spirit-filled Scottish Bible teacher, called Albert Leckie whose knowledge of God's Word I have not seen equaled, anywhere. (A second cousin of Edward Heath's, in fact). He told me it once happened to him and the congregation would not go home, but just sat on. It was happening to us. When eventually we did close the meeting in prayer is it any wonder that amongst those converted was the girl for whom her father had wept sore in prayer on the Saturday? I am not advocating emotionalism, but what I am emphasising is brokenness in the presence of our God. He is not some theological nicety. He is alive and real and ready to bless. But, we must have a 'Gethsemane experience' as His blessed Son did if we are to have His fellowship. 'Not my will - but Thine be done!'

She was only a gleaner amidst alien corn. A lovely girl whose lover had died and living amongst people she did not know. Humble, insignificant and broken. Her back bending to pull at but strands of what others were getting arm loads. It was all that was allowed to her, but God had sent her there. He knew what He was doing; 'who never negligently yet fashioned an April violet'. She was in the right corner of the field. It may have been a path of brokenness, but it was the path of blessing. In fact, though she was not fully aware of it, it was the path of God.

Across the will of nature,
Leads on the path of God;
Not where the flesh delighteth
The feet of Jesus trod.

0 bliss to leave behind us
The fetter of the slave,
To leave ourselves behind us,
The grave clothes and the grave!

We follow in His footsteps:
What if our feet be torn?
Where He has marked the pathway
All hail the brier and thorn!

Scarce seen, scarce heard, unreckoned,
Despised, defamed, unknown
Or heard but by our saying,
On, children, ever on!

Fields take cultivation,
but it must come slow,
unhurried by the tractor's tread.
Good farmers don't harass the ground
 until the ground is ready.
And just as only experts
have the means to teach us hate,
farming is an art form too.

So whether planting love
or lima beans
the careful man goes carefully
down his furrows.

- Rod McKuen

$\mathscr{L}$OVE

HE ALWAYS RUBBED HIS FINGER UP AND DOWN THE RAISED BOOK REST ON HIS DESK. WHEN EMPHASISING a point he would look over his half-rimmed glasses and catch the head of a small nail on the side of his book rest and squeeze it between his finger and thumb.

I studied his every move because I sat at the desk right at the front of his English class. Norman Watts officially, but to us, privately, he was always Nore. And we loved him.

My pal Cunningham and I used to vie with each other to see who would get the highest marks for 'Nore's Essay' set every other weekend. Dear help (it is an Irish expression) Nore if Cunningham got one more mark than I! We always wanted to know why.

Legends surrounded him in school: most of them were true. He was parachuted into France as a soldier in wartime and walked the length of the land as a Polish farmer! Despite the legends he opened our minds as youngsters to the beauty of words.

I can see him yet with the backdrop of Downpatrick Cathedral and the sun filtering the dust in the room and streaming in the window as Nore would say: 'Now watch this word boys. Keats always uses the right word on the right occasion: no other word will do. You cannot find a better description of a glass of wine than "beaded bubble winking at the brim". Or on Hamlet, "when Shakespeare makes ghosts walk - ghosts walk! ..."' He brought the very best out of you.

The point is that it was Nore who first introduced me to the language of love in poetry. Not old sentiment, but the real thing in words. We will always remember the words of Browning's 'Meeting at Night' as Nore taught it. 'Listen to the sound coming out in the words boys,' he would say...

The grey sea and the long black land;
And the yellow half-moon large and low;
And the startled little waves that leap
In fiery ringlets from their sleep,
As I gain the cove with pushing prow,
And quench its speed in the slushy sand.

Then a mile of warm sea-scented beach;
Three fields to cross till a farm appears;
A tap at the pane, the quick sharp scratch
And blue spurt of a lighted match,
And a voice less loud, thro' its joy and fears,
Than the two hearts beating each to each!

It is that last line which is gentle on my mind when I think of Boaz and Ruth. Two hearts beating each to each? It certainly was love at first sight, and 'Behold,' says the author of Ruth, as if he were adding a fresh touch of vividness to his writing. Behold what? A man has arrived on the scene. No mean man. Wealthy, some even translate it 'A mighty man of valour.' According to Leon Morris, we get the force of it by thinking of our word 'Knight'. It seems that added to his money he was a man of great moral worth and his name means 'Strength'. It is no alien harvest he has come to supervise - it is his own ! 'The Lord be with you' he says to the reapers. He knows the Lord too ! What girl would not pray for such a combination in a man; wealthy, full of moral worth, a man of strength (strong, silent type!) and in love with the Lord? Blessed combination.

The eyes of the great man rove the field checking out his workers when suddenly they stop at - Ruth! 'Whose damsel is this?' he asks a servant, and the news is not long in coming back. The thing about his servant's answer is that he must have had his eye on Ruth all day because his report was that the young woman (damsel) was the one that came back with Naomi and that she had 'continued even from the morning until now, that she tarried a little in the house.' That simply means that he had even noticed the break she had taken in the house, probably adjacent to the field being reaped. She was being watched.

Now comes the blessing. Somebody had heard of her plight, though she did not know it. Walking quietly up to her, Boaz lays his blessing upon her young life. He had heard of her faithfulness. He knew of the separation from her father, mother and the land of her nativity. He knew that she had come unto a people 'which thou knewest not.' He knew it and he told her so.

Best of all, he recognised that the Lord God of Israel was the One 'under whose wings thou art come to trust'. He tells her to go to no other field. If thirsty, she is to drink of the water his young men have drawn and warned the same young men not to touch her. Why that warning? The single reason is that the enthusiasm of gleaners sometimes carried them beyond their allotted area; they came too close to the reapers, annoyed them and they were sometimes forced to drive them back. Ruth was not to be touched. She was to be left alone. And more, much more. At mealtime she sat by the reapers, dipped her bread in vinegar and Boaz handed her parched corn, 'and she did eat, and was sufficed.' Parched corn? As W. M. Thompson points out in his book 'The Land of the Book'; 'A quantity of the best ears, not too ripe are plucked with the stalks attached. These are tied into small parcels, a blazing fire is kindled with dry grass and thorn bushes, and the corn heads are held in it until the chaff is mostly burned off. The grain is thus sufficiently roasted to be eaten, and it is a favourite article all over the country.' She goes back to her work and Boaz tells his young men to 'let fall some of the handfuls of purpose for her,' as an extra thrown in.

When writing this last paragraph I received a telephone call from a very dedicated Christian woman known to all and sundry as Peggy. She is a very wonderful mother of seven children and is a fund of knowledge on everything from a needle to how to handle preachers ! When I am on a writing spree she rings me up to see how things are going and to pass on her thought for the day. Today's was particularly apt. 'Did you ever think about that verse which says "My God shall supply all your need according to his riches in glory by Christ Jesus"?' she asked me over a telephone line that connected one hundred miles of Ireland that lay between us. I said I had. 'Did you notice it says, supply all your NEED. That simply means you don't get the supply until you have the need!' What a very obvious but profound thought. As each need arises, He supplies it. You didn't get that prayer answered because the Lord did not feel that today was the time you needed it answered. He never keeps anything in His plan for your life that you need now. God's supply and demand system is different to ours. The prodigal son grabs all and runs, but when the world's supply proves that there is a hole in the bucket and he discovers he needs his father's love and care, behold, there it is!

God is like that. The whole world was lost in the darkness of sin. Mankind was separated from Him; there was no mediator. Then at the very time when we were without strength, God acted. He saw our need. We were strangers from the Commonwealth of Israel and the Covenants of Promise. Like Ruth we were picking up just what we could find and not making much of it.

We were thirsting and we knew that we could not live by bread alone. Lonely, searching, and heading for trouble. God's love spotted us. He sent that Precious Baby to Bethlehem. He led Him through childhood to manhood. His will was to do His Father's will and that led to the depths of Gethsemane, the journey to the judgment hall and the darkness of Calvary. When we were without strength, Christ died for us ! When we were Godless, Christ died for the ungodly! God loved the world -good. Christ loved the Church - better. But the Son of God who loved ME and gave Himself for me - absolutely supreme! No person was ever born again of the Spirit of God without first learning their need of Him! When, by faith, we discover that our need is supplied.

Our sins were not only forgiven, but this heavenly Boaz did much more! He quenched our thirst. I love F. B. Meyer's commentary on John 4 and the woman at the well. He says:

> '... Whosoever drinketh of this water, shall thirst again' is a legend that might be engraved on Jacob's well: and equally in every theatre, and other place of worldly amusement or sin, the votaries of which get sips, not draughts; but this would satisfy. In the failure of human love, in the absence of blessed friendships and companionships, in the subsidence of every Cherith brook, those who received what He longed to bestow should never thirst'.

May we in turn,

As from far untrodden snow
Of Lebanon the streams run free,
Dear Lord, command our streams to flow,
That thirsty men may drink of Thee.

Then of course He gave us bread - fed us until we wanted no more. Like Ruth, 'we were sufficed.' No wonder we fall at His feet, and like Ruth say 'Why have I found grace in thine eyes, that thou shouldst take knowledge of me, seeing I am a stranger?' Why did the Lord Jesus pick me out? Why you? Why, when millions in this modern age rush on to eternity with no thought of spiritual things, did the Lord Jesus by His Spirit find me in the field ('the field is the world,' Mark 4) and give me food, drink, and set me in His banqueting house and His banner over me was love?

Then, as if that were not enough, He drops handfuls of purpose for me along the way. Why? My dear reader, if I could answer that question I would be God. 'I know not why, I only cry, Oh, how He loves me!'

I may be wrong, but I strongly suspect that Boaz was deeply in love from the very first glance. Is there anything wrong with that?

Though cities bow to art, and I am its own true lover,
It is not art, but heart, which wins the wide world over.

Dr. Boreham once wrote of an eminent pianist whose recitals crowded the most spacious auditoriums in Europe with ecstatic audiences. Yet there was just one thing lacking in his life. This brilliant pianist was a lonely, taciturn man and a certain coldness and aloofness would steal into his playing from time to time. At that time there also lived another much older pianist whose name was a household word in musical circles the wide world over. One day this person laid their hand upon the shoulder of the brilliant younger performer and said: 'Will you let me tell you, my boy, that your playing lacks one thing. So far you have missed the greatest thing in the world. And, unless you fall in love, there will always be a certain cold perfection about your music. Unless you come to love another human being passionately and unselfishly, you will never touch human hearts as deeply as you might.'

As in the natural and physical, so in the spiritual. Methinks I detect in my Christian service a very similar 'coldness and aloofness.' Mechanical, technical, theological - but dry. Often it is because my love for my Lord has grown very cold. As someone once said 'we take it for granted that we preach Christ because we love Christ'; but is the assumption always safe? It was many

centuries ago that one of the greatest Christians who ever lived wrote
from a prison cell:

> 'If I had the gift of being able to speak in other
> languages without learning them, and could
> speak in every language there is in all of heaven
> and earth, but didn't love others, I would only be
> making noise. If I had the gift of prophecy and
> knew all about what is going to happen in the
> future, knew everything about everything, but
> didn't love others, what good would it do? Even
> if I had the gift of faith so that I could speak to
> a mountain and make it move, I would still
> be worth nothing at all without love. If I gave
> everything I have to poor people, and if I were
> burned alive for preaching the Gospel but didn't
> love others, it would be of no value whatever.'
> 'Love is very patient and kind, never jealous or
> envious, never boastful or proud, never haughty
> or selfish or rude. Love does not demand its own
> way. It is not irritable or touchy. It does not
> hold grudges and will hardly even notice when
> others do it wrong. It is never glad about
> injustice, but rejoices whenever truth wins out.
> If you love someone you will be loyal to him no
> matter what the cost. You will always believe in
> him, always expect the best of him, and always
> stand your ground in defending him.'
> 'All the special gifts and powers from God will
> some day come to an end, but love goes on for
> ever.'

Mere sentiment - no sir!

I sometimes remind myself of the story Catherine Marshall
tells about the dream she had about her husband Peter. She was

discussing with her husband the biography of his life that she was occupied in writing when he laid down a condition. What was the condition? 'Tell the world, Catherine, that a man can love the Lord and not be a cissy!' I like it.

> *It's the heart where the summer is molded*
> *And woven the magical blue,*
> *And always a glory is folded*
> *That waits but a welcome from you.*
> *The world is the world that you make it,*
> *A dungeon, a desert, a bower;*
> *The sunshine is falling and cuckoos are*
> *calling*
> *If only the heart is in flower.*

When the Rose of Sharon blooms there - all is well!

$\mathcal{A}$T $\mathcal{H}$IS $\mathcal{F}$EET

I HAVE DISCOVERED A STRANGE THING. SOMETIMES
WHENEVER FEET AND THE LORD JESUS ARE MENTIONED
in the New Testament, there is criticism. Mary sat at His feet and
was scolded by Martha. Another Mary poured ointment on His feet
and was scolded by the Pharisees. Jesus went to wash the disciples'
feet and was scolded by Peter.

Let us, for a second, look at this phenomenon.

My mother was not a philosopher or a great theologian in terms
of the great women in the history of the Church. Her name will not
be found in the annals of some great library, but as far as I and those
who were privileged to be near to her were concerned, the spiritual
things she taught us will be forever in our hearts. Her name was
written in Heaven when one day as a girl she accepted the Lord
Jesus as her Saviour and that's what REALLY mattered to her. One
day she came running into my room, Bible in hand. 'Look at this,'
she exclaimed. Look at what? 'The story of Mary and Martha.'

For twenty minutes she sat down and poured out some gleanings she had gained from her quiet reading of the story. My mum had little time for commentaries and read little but pure scripture. The point she emphasised to me that day was what Jesus said of Mary, who sat at His feet. He said that she had 'chosen that better part, which shall not be taken away from her'! Looking at me with determination mother declared: 'Shall not be taken away in time or eternity! To sit at Jesus feet is an eternal blessing! What you gain there you simply cannot lose. It goes on with you forever. It will NEVER be taken away from you, son!'

As I sit here writing today I think of my mother, lying, dying of cancer. After a life of unending faithfulness to her Lord, her evangelist husband, and to us as boys, she has to face - this! Anybody who has ever lived in a house with a cancer patient will know what I am talking about. Deadly enemy!

About a week before she died I remember coming in from school teaching, and after throwing my books down I gently knocked on her door. Standing at the bottom of her bed, I faced her square.

'Now mother, honestly tell me. Are you afraid to die? You may think it a strange question, but at this stage of your life, is the Lord Jesus as real to you as when you were without pain? I have got to know.'

She pointed to the lovely text on the wall above her which two dedicated Christian nurses had given her:

'"Thou shalt keep him in *perfect peace* whose mind is stayed upon thee." That is what I have got', she said.

Now tell me, where did my mother originally get that peace? She got it one day by faith, as a ten-year-old girl kneeling at the sore wounded feet of a living Christ. She used to tell me over and over again that she had no great vision, no text, no preacher near her, but in trusting Him she got peace. The burden went. As we laid her in the cemetery, I could not forget her words to me:

'Shall not be taken away! ... in time or eternity. To sit at Jesus feet is an eternal blessing! What you gain there you simply cannot lose. It goes on with you forever. It will NEVER be taken away from you, son!' I can see her in glory enjoying it now.

In Luke seven we read of a nameless woman who had not a reputation that was fragrant. 'A woman in the city which was a sinner,' says Luke. What caused her to stand behind the Son of God, weeping, would interest me greatly. Did she see that Simon, the Pharisee, had not even had the courtesy to offer water for His hot and tired feet? Did her heart not move within her as she saw the callousness of the men who cared so much for the letter of the law and were very careless about the Master of it? I wish I had words to grip the meaning of the phrase, 'She stood at His feet weeping,' yet she did not stand long because soon she was on her knees and was wiping those feet with the hairs of her head, kissing them and anointing them with oil. He is, you see, the sinners' Saviour. The religious nation of Israel pierced His feet with nails, but a sinful woman kissed them. He came not to call the righteous but sinners to repentance. Simon thought only of the outward, for he reckoned a woman of her calibre could only be capable of one thing. He was wrong - what she was doing would never be taken away from her, for the same principle applies to her as applied to the other Mary. How? Did not Jesus say, 'Wheresoever the gospel shall be preached in the whole world, there shall also this, that this woman hath done, be told for a *memorial* to her.' It shall not be taken away from her. You see, getting down at Jesus feet involves the low place. He becomes the focus of all that we do, our directions come from Him. When you abandon yourself to that position, look out, for the devil will be on your track. He was on Mary's, but she cared not. There is the place of power. To sit and learn of Him, to saturate your mind and heart with his humility and fragrance. There is true success.

Ruth got there. Quietly, stealthily, she walked down to the threshing-floor. The Bible says she went down and I would take that simply to mean that Bethlehem was ridged and normally although one would go up to a threshing-floor, she had to go down to the building in order to climb. It was night and no one saw her. She had bathed (lit. meaning of 'wash' in the text), anointed herself and went down to where Boaz lay sleeping on the threshing-floor. Not a sound was heard as she quietly uncovered his feet of the cloak that covered them, and lay down, at the end of 'the heap of corn'. Not a stir. She lay there gently, quietly, waiting.

Now I fully realise that this is a most difficult point. It is amazing how expositors of the Bible always fight shy of questions on the chapter. I have asked quite a few, and they just pass this action off as 'custom', and will not be drawn any further. Some custom! It certainly was not attested other than here. Was she not going too far? Was she pushing this man's gentleness?

No, I do not believe it. It will take a little explanation, Naomi's plans in sending Ruth to the threshing-floor certainly had its dangers, but she obviously trusted her. As we shall see, she had a right to be there. Yet interwoven into this story is the great scriptural thread of God's brinkmanship. Let me explain.

In Israel when a man died it was decreed that the brother of the deceased was to marry the widow. If he refused then the woman could publicly humiliate him. Naomi probably knew that there was another kinsman other than Boaz, but calculated that he would not redeem Ruth so she reckoned on introducing Ruth to Boaz first. Boaz was, of course, directly related to Naomi and was in line to redeem Ruth's seed. So that young woman lying at the feet of Boaz was showing him by her action that she was willing to be redeemed. Whether her action was right or wrong, she was staking her claim. She wanted the redemption which he could offer, and she lay at his feet and was waiting to see what he would do. She took the lowest place.

We have come across the word 'Behold' in this story before, and here it is again. The first time was when his eyes fell on Ruth, the second was 'and it came to pass at midnight, that the man was afraid, and turned himself, and, behold, a woman lay at his feet.' Behold indeed! When Ruth gives her identity and reminds him that he is a 'near kinsman', it soon becomes obvious that a great moment had arrived. Let us hold it there a moment.

God had promised in the very beginning, after sin entered our universe, to send His Son into the world. Did you ever stop to think how it often seemed as though He was going to break His promise? When the huge floods burst on the earth and a boat held eight people out of the whole of earth's population it did not look as though the coming Messiah was going to come from that line. Yet, they were preserved. Talk about brinkmanship! When God promised Abram that through his seed all the nations of the earth would be blessed it certainly did not look like it when he was asked to raise his knife and slay Isaac. Yet, there was a ram caught in the thicket. Talk about brinkmanship! Six feet of air between a knife and death.

Then there were Israel's escapes. The number of times when it was only a lonely man on Sinai called Moses that pleaded with God to preserve them, would amaze you. Count them sometime. But then, one with God is a majority. The line was preserved yet again.

To think of Ruth quietly claiming her right to be redeemed on a threshing-floor in Bethlehem as, though she did not know it, actually preserving the line of the Messiah, is a tremendous moment in this great story.

Take Hezekiah when God told him to set his house in order for he was to die and not live. He turned his head to the wall and wept, pleading with God to preserve him. He was given fifteen extra years and in that time a son was born to him, who carried on that Royal line. Why does God sometimes move to the very brink?

It is God's nature to show that the wisdom of men is but foolishness with Him. Man delights in showing his wisdom, but God delights in hiding things from the wise and prudent and revealing them unto babes. Like a quiet, insignificant, peasant girl called Mary, for instance, locked out of an inn, though expecting a little one. Given no place in the eyes of men, just one in a crowd, yet given by God the greatest privilege ever given to womanhood: to give birth to the Prince of Peace. God does not act in some great fanfare - He uses humble, obedient people, one here, one there, because He

'Hath chosen the foolish things of the world
To confound the wise,
... the weak things of the world,

To confound the mighty.
... base things of the world ... which are despised,
Things which are not to bring to naught things that are,
That no flesh should glory in His presence.'

Greatest of all, is Calvary; so despised by the world Darkness, seeming defeat, weak in the eyes of men. The world thought it was the end of the road, but little did they realise that it was the greatest victory ever won. No wonder Paul (I like sometimes to call him Mr. Greatheart!) said: 'For though He was crucified through weakness, yet He liveth by the power of God!' Tell me, reader, have you been to Calvary? Have you repented of your sin and put your trust in the precious blood shed there for your sin. It is the blood of Jesus Christ, His Son, that cleanseth us from all sin. It seems weak in human terms, but, as Paul adds, 'We also are weak WITH (margin) Him, but we shall live with Him by the power of God towards you.' In Christ we have everything, without Him, nothing.

At His feet! Do you despise that place? Maybe a Christian reader is feeling despised because of the seemingly insignificant role you have been given by the Lord. Could I quote to you a beautiful piece of writing which means a lot to me? I don't know where I found it, I don't know who wrote it, but here it is:

> 'I was tired and sat down under the shadow of the great pines in a Swedish forest, glad to find such a cool retreat from the broiling sun. I had not been there long before I noticed a fragrant odour and wondered what it could be and where it came from.
>
> 'No Marechal Niel rose grew on that barren soil, nor could the sun penetrate the shades of the forest to extract its perfume even if it had; I looked round, and found by my side a tiny flower about half the size of an ordinary daisy, nearly hidden from view by the moss. It was the little "Linea blomma".

'Oh, how fragrant it smelt! Again and again I held it near my face, enjoying the perfume, and then I looked up and thanked God for that tiny flower so insignificant, growing in a wild, almost untrodden forest, yet bringing cheer and refreshment to me.

'I thought, why is it so obscure, when it is a flower with such fragrance, and surely worthy of a place in the most stately grounds? I learned a lesson by it, and it spoke powerfully to my heart.

"I thought, if I cannot be a pine in God's forest, I may be a tiny flower to send forth the fragrance of Jesus in this world of sadness.'

There is a tendency in our hearts to desire to be or to do something great. We may not be content, like the tiny linea flower, to send forth fragrance in obscurity.

I have often met the Lord's people despondent over the apparent uselessness of their lives. They cannot point to some great feat accomplished for the Lord. It has never been theirs to figure prominently in His service, nor have they the remembrance of having done anything worthy of the record.

It is written, 'Seekest thou great things for thy self? seek them not' (Jer. 45:5). Beloved fellow believers, let me tell you it is possible for you to be fragrant in this world. Keep close to Christ, walk in happy communion with Him; let your heart drink in His love and you will be fragrant to Him.

Could you conceive anything greater than that? No eye may see you but His, no ear hear you but His, no heart appreciate your act or thought but His; yet how precious, I can be fragrant to the Lord Jesus! Nothing surely is so delightful to Him as to have you and me walking with Himself. If this is so, we shall also surely come in contact with some weary soul who needs refreshment. We can speak of Jesus, and in such a way that there will be a Christ-likeness about us. Let us give up the disappointing business of self-occupation. As long as we are occupied with self, we are not occupied with Christ. True greatness is the measure in which the excellence of Christ flows forth from us.

'His name is as ointment poured forth.' He was not great as men count greatness. He chose no place of prominence. When by force they would make Him king, He retired; when His brethren pressed Him to go up to the feast to do some great miracle and make Himself prominent, He answered, 'My time is not yet come.'

To do His Father's will was His one commanding business. Oh! that 'Plant of renown', that 'Branch of David's stem', that 'Root out of a dry ground', who could say: 'All my springs are in thee.'

What fragrance came forth from Him! Those who were far from God could smell the holy perfume, and say: 'Never man spake like this man.' The heartless Pilate had to say, 'I find no fault in this man.' The centurion at the cross had to confess, 'Certainly this was a righteous man.' Others could but marvel at 'the gracious words that proceeded out of his mouth.'

None could come into His presence without smelling the fragrant odours of love, compassion and tenderness. The wickedness of the human heart, which He met on every hand, only disclosed His preciousness more and more. Let us then not be despondent over what we are and what we are not. Let our attention be more than ever directed to Him, so that as He fills our vision everything else may vanish. As His sweetness fills the soul, so will His fragrance flow forth from us as the outcome of communion with Him.

May the Lord, then, so attach your hearts to Himself that, like the little Linea flower, sending forth its odour in the untrodden forest, we may send forth by His Spirit and for His own pleasure something of His fragrance, in this world where He is not, and so become a reflection of the only perfect and fragrant One, Jesus!

God of the heights, austere, inspiring,
Thy word hath come to me,
0 let no selfish aims conspiring

Distract my soul from Thee.
Loosen me from things of time,
Strengthen me for steadfast climb.

The temporal would bind my spirit;
Father, be Thou my stay.
Show me what flesh cannot inherit
Stored for another day.
Be transparent, things of time.
Looking through you, I would climb.

Now by Thy grace my spirit chooseth,
Treasure that shall abide.
The great unseen, I know, endureth,
My footsteps shall not slide.
Not for me the things of time,
God of the mountain, I will climb.

$\mathscr{A}$ $\mathscr{M}$AN'S $\mathscr{R}$EACTION

HAVE YOU EVER SEEN A ROUND PEG TRYING TO GET IN A SQUARE HOLE? IT HAPPENS EVERY DAY. THE SPEAKER rises to speak with the words, 'Now I'm no speaker . . . but.' Twenty minutes later (or even less) it is obvious to everybody that he is just exactly what he said he was - no speaker. Much better to be thought a fool than to open your mouth and remove all doubt! Great cooks being waiters when they should be in the kitchen, young men who love and were brought up to love farming and wide open spaces spending their days in a stuffy city office because they think that is the way to sophistication. Thousands of people in the wrong jobs!

Yet to see a man doing his job who really knows how to do it is a beautiful thing to watch. The craftsman at the potter's wheel; the natural teacher bending over a pupil with a problem; the dedicated, happy, doctor tickling his little child patient and giving it a reassuring smile and goading it back to health; the strong arm of the gifted, spiritual pastor as he gently leads a wayward Christian back onto a better path; the gifted evangelist as he burns the flame of his message before the thoughtless men of the world in language they understand; the gifted, gentle, Bible teacher as he unravels the gems of God's word and feeds the flock instead of flogging them.

We all know gift when we see it. Gift does not need to trumpet to draw attention to its qualities. It is as clear as day. Gift always makes way for itself. You have a gift given you of God - use it! Don't, for any sake, try to be somebody else.

> *Whatever you are- be that,*
> *Whatever you say - be true,*
> *Straightforwardly act- be honest, in fact*
> *Be nobody else but you.*

Boaz, to me at least, was a natural. I imagine him to be the kind of person you could go to when in trouble. Gentle, warm, sensitive. Always beware of the man who is hard in spirit - he is usually hiding something. I can see another man reacting in the situation Boaz found himself in.

A young woman, beautiful Ruth, lay at his feet, claiming marriage. It was night. No one had seen her come. They were alone. Yet, here was no silly old fool. Here was no village lout. Here was a gentleman. Boaz, who had at the very roots of his manly nature the two rare qualities of twentieth century men, dignity and restraint.

Gently he talks to Ruth in the quietness and stillness, his accent calming her fears. Spiritual and manly.

'Blessed be thou of the Lord, my daughter; for thou hast shewed more kindness in the latter end than at the beginning ... I will do all that thou requirest for all the city of my people know that thou art a virtuous woman.'

It was her sense of the RIGHT that impressed him. She had not followed after other men, whether rich or poor. Boaz was in line to redeem her, and to Boaz she came.

By his very definition of Ruth as 'a virtuous woman' he certainly shows that as far as he was concerned there was no impropriety in what Ruth had done. Before she leaves, Boaz asks her to hold her cloak out and into it he measures eighty pounds of barley!

His gift was love and care: he showed it perfectly. What if he had refused? What if he had turned her away? There was no sign of it. He was not ashamed of her.

It is not, of course, within my powers to adequately describe the Lord Jesus who was not ashamed of me when I came to Him for redemption. Many pens have tried and failed. What if He had not fulfilled His promise ?

What if He let me lie there? Yet He did not. He not only filled my cloak with plenty but He gave His precious blood to redeem me. Did you ever try to think of just how precious that blood was?

Robert McLuckie is a most lovable Scotsman; to the core, in fact. He even claims that Scotland is God's very own country! One day he took me for a walk around Edinburgh Castle and glowed as he described the historical background of Edinburgh Castle and tradition of his land as symbolised in that great citadel. By and by he took me into the throne room, and there in a casket lay the crown jewels of Scotland. The central crown really drew my attention and turning to the assistant who stood by with his long coat and many buttons I queried, 'How much is it worth?'

I was amazed at his reaction. He was flaming angry. 'How much is it worth?' he reiterated. 'Yes, thirty million, forty million. Surely there must be some price on it?' 'Young man,' he said emphatically, 'three thousand men died in one day to put that crown on the head of Robert the Bruce. If you want to put a price upon human blood you are welcome to try. The crown is priceless!' As he defused, and Robert and I beat a hasty retreat, my friend smiled at me when we were at a safe distance and said, 'You've got a sermon there, lad!' He was right. 'If you want to put a price upon human blood you are welcome to try'. Surely if we cannot attempt to put a price upon the blood of Scotsmen who died in battle, how, just how, can we put a price on that precious blood that stained the hill of Calvary? Divine life, became human life that we might have everlasting life. The answer is simple - it is priceless, and Peter put it this way: 'For we are not redeemed with corruptible things such as silver and gold, but with the precious blood of Christ as of a lamb without blemish and without spot.' That was the price of redemption for us: nothing less would satisfy God, and it does. Doesn't it satisfy you?

It is there that the rest of the true Christian comes. He made peace through the blood of His cross. Rest is one of the key words in the book of Ruth. Naomi sent Ruth to Boaz with the question 'Shall I not seek rest for thee, that it may be well with thee?' She sent her to the right man. Tell me, where do you go for rest? Do you go where so many young folk go in this generation? For an hour I talked to a fellow the other night who longed for rest and the ultimate. He was given some drugs at a beach party on one of our nearby beaches and he found his rest all right - for about an hour. He soon woke up with a craving for more and more and ... Months later, as a broken, brain stormed lad he admitted to me that it could not satisfy. Try them all. Drink. Permissiveness. Entertainment. They all fail - but the Lord Jesus, never! He does what drugs or anything else can never do. Like another drug-taker I came into contact with recently. In the middle of the night he wandered into our room where we were working and pointed a line out of a book to us. It was one of Arthur Blessitt's books where Arthur had been quoting from the Bible. What did it say? This: 'New creature in Christ Jesus ...'

'I want that,' he said. He was looking in the right direction.

Ruth, carrying her burden, now returns home. Eagerness describes her conversation as she pours out all that has happened to her mother-in-law, yet, I suspect Ruth suffered from a very common modern complaint - nerves! Is it too good to be true? The questions arise in her heart. Is he really going to redeem me? The reason I pose these questions is simply because her mother-in-law began to gently upbraid her. 'Sit still, my daughter, until thou know how the matter will fall...' Sit still, relax!

Doubt is one of the greatest enemies of the Christian. I have yet to meet a man who has not had an attack of doubt at some stage. In the problems of human life there come those moments when people begin to doubt, especially when things go wrong. They put their trust in the Lord Jesus but, like Peter, when by the various circumstances of life their eyes go from Him, they begin to sink. The doubting castle of Bunyan's day is just as solid today. Intellectual doubts. Young people questioning everything. Their teachers teaching them to doubt sometimes. Why, I lunched with a Bavarian doctor this very day who told me that the man in his 'church' pulpit did not believe in eternal life! It was pretty obvious to me that he knew nothing about it. Europe may seem to breed doubters, but amidst it all there are those whose faith is resting in the Rock of Ages. They believe that theirs is not an unreasonable faith but that it is beyond reason. What word could be given to the true believers who are in Doubting Castle? Just this! Naomi has a word for Ruth.

'Sit still ... *for* the man will not be in rest until he has finished the thing this day.' If Boaz said he would do it, then he would do it. If God says He will save you if you trust His Son, then He will do just that. If God says 'Delight thyself also in the Lord and he shall give thee the desires of thine heart,' He will not rest until it is done. While we stumble and stray here, the Lord never rests working for us. While Ruth worried, Boaz was in the city busy knocking down the problems, one by one!

Our God neither slumbers nor sleeps. Away, young person with your doubting - He shall not rest until He has finished the thing for you, this day! Did Karl Marx ever reach down and give you peace? Have existentialists like Jean Paul Satre ever given you one minute's rest of mind and heart? You can philosophise, argue, call it relativity, conditioning or anything else you like to call it, but one thing I know - once I was restless, purposeless, empty and lost, now I have, the Lord Jesus. Like you, maybe, I too have sat listening to hundreds of lectures given by the greatest of minds, but they never, ever, gave me what I got through the victory of Calvary - a Holy

Spirit to guide me, a salvation to save me, and a Christ to redeem me. I do not understand all this; do not begin to understand it; never expect to understand it. Yet I realise that it meets the deepest needs of my heart.

For a thousand reasons I feel that I am but a little child, and need a Father; I am a sinful man and I desperately need a Saviour; I am troubled and heartbroken, and I need the Spirit, the Comforter. If He shall not rest, day or night, working at God's right hand on our behalf, then what cause have we to fear? Sit still!

One final thing. There is another question which Christian young people in particular are always asking - I want this or that desperately and the Lord does not answer me. If He shall not rest concerning me, what's holding Him up on the answer? I was in a newspaper editor's office the other day and someone had stuck on the very desk in front of me this verse that we are talking about. Girls in particular seem to hold on to the promise, but think the Lord is slow on answering. To you I can only quote a favourite poem. To Ruth the Lord said 'yes' on this particular issue; to you -

Just a lovely little child,
Three years old,
And a mother with a heart
All of gold,
Often did that mother say
Jesus hears us when we pray,
For He's never far away,
And He always answers.

Now that tiny little child
Had brown eyes,
And she wanted blue instead,
Like blue skies,
For her mother's eyes were blue,
Like forget-me-nots. She knew
All her mother said was true,
Jesus always answered.

So she prayed for two blue eyes,
Said 'Goodnight',
Went to sleep in deep content,
And delight.
Woke up early, climbed a chair.
By a mirror. Where, 0 where
Could the blue eyes be? not there;
Jesus hadn't answered.

Hadn't answered her at all;
Never more
Could she pray; her eyes were brown
As before.
Did a little soft wind blow?
Came a whisper soft and low,
Jesus answered. He said 'No';
Isn't No an answer?

'ᔐILL ᔐAPPINESS ᔐTEPS Uᑭ ᔐO ᔐREET ᔐE

'If we saw the whole, we should see that the Father is doing little else in the world but training His vines.'
ROBERT MURRAY McCHEYNE

DO YOU BELIEVE THAT EVERYTHING THAT HAPPENS TO YOU IS IN A PLAN? EVERYTHING? THE MISTAKES ALONG with the success? The tears that blind along with the pounding heart? The days when you could rip your telephone out of the wall and the days when you could ring the whole world. The times when those children of yours drive you into despair and the days you could cuddle the life out of them. The cycle of life: marriage - birth - death. Is every second, minute, hour, day, month, year, decade of your life part of a plan outside of yourself and directed by the God of Eternity?

For the Christian, the answer is yes, if the rules we talked about in chapter two are obeyed. If we are not guided by the Lord and know that ALL things work together for good to them that love Him, the whole point of following Him would be pretty hopeless. But why, before God can bring Ruth to the place of security, rest and happiness did she have to go through so much? This chapter deals with the success of God's great plan, for all God's plans are successful, but why must we have to walk through fields of alien corn first?

Ellice Hopkins once put it this way:

> 'Do you know the lovely fact about the opal? That, in the first place, it is made only of a desert dust, sand, silica, and owes its beauty and preciousness to a defect. It is a stone with a broken heart. It is full of minute fissures which admit air, and the air reflects the light. Hence its lovely hues, and that sweet lamp of fire that ever burns at its heart, for the breath of the Lord God is in it.
> 'You are only conscious of the cracks and desert dust, but so He makes His precious opal. We must be broken in ourselves before we can give back the lovely hues of His light, and the lamp in the temple can burn in us and never go out.'

We have dealt with this subject of brokenness before in this book, but before we tell of Ruth in her bliss let us remember the long, difficult path that led up to it. It is you see, my friend Ernie Shanks who is continually reminding me of it. Ernie has, at this time of writing, no kidneys. He had them both removed recently and awaits a transplant. I went to see him to try and bring him some comfort the other day. The intensive care unit was most foreboding; all who entered must be clothed from head to toe with protecting garments to shield Ernie from germs.

Slipping a small Bible into my garment I went in and sat beside his bed. Yet, a strange thing occurred. I did not do the talking: he did. Inspiration did not come from me - it came from him. The radiant smile was not on my face - it was on his.

When, eventually, he left hospital and I got him to take part in some evangelistic meetings, it was Ernie who had the power. I took an unconverted socialite to one of those meetings and he was so impressed he rang up the hospital when he got home from the meeting and offered them his kidney! When Ernie rises to speak, people sit up and listen. I have seen him lead a great congregation in singing and hardly a dry eye in the place. Why such power? Why is Ernie 'on fire' for the Lord Jesus? Simply because, like the opal, he owes the beauty and fragrance of his life to a defect that he left in the hands of His Master and is content to leave it there. Some of us with no physical defects are miserable. Lord, set us on fire, but help us to be content to go through alien corn first, whatever it costs - like Ernie!

There were ten elders at the gate of the city that day surrounded by a speculative crowd, for the whole world loves a lover. It must have been a heart-throbbing scene for Ruth as her redeemer stands looking at the man next in line to redeem her. He is called in Biblical terms, the kinsman. He is unmarried and, I judge, significantly. Boaz points out to him that Naomi has a piece of land to sell which he has a right to buy. Would he redeem it? He was willing.

Now Boaz comes to the crux of the matter. Ruth, the Moabitess as well as Naomi, is concerned with this field. If the kinsman is to redeem the field then this involves marrying Ruth, the widow of a childless kinsman in order to have a child to carry on the inheritance. In other words if he is to buy the field then he must in addition provide for Ruth. The problem was there before him. It is obvious that the kinsman was certainly ready to buy the field without marrying Ruth, and he may well have been even ready to marry Ruth without buying the field. What he could not face was doing the two things. It would mar his inheritance. 'I cannot redeem it,' he says. I leave you to conjecture why. He certainly was not willing to redeem all that she was and had.

Not so Boaz. I can see the kinsman, according to ancient custom, drawing off his shoe, and handing it to Boaz to indicate the withdrawal of his claim to redeem and inviting Boaz to take it up ! What a moment in our story as the crowd gather at the gate of the city to watch this amazing transaction - for the gate of a city in Judah tended to become the very centre of city life. The words ring out clear and plain as the redeemer makes his great speech:

> 'Ye are witnesses this day, that I have bought all
> that was Elimelech's, and all that was Chilion's
> and Mahlon's, of the hand of Naomi. Moreover
> Ruth the Moabitess, the wife of Mahlon, have I
> purchased to be my wife, to raise up the name of
> the dead upon his inheritance, that the name of
> the dead be not cut off from among his brethren,
> and from the gate of his place: ye are witnesses
> this day.'

The emphasis I would draw here would lie on that phrase - 'I have bought all that was Elimelech's, and all that was Chilion's and Mahlon's, of the hand of Naomi ... Moreover Ruth.' Let us not forget that this great story of love was written for our learning. This book fits perfectly into the great pattern of God's divine revelation to man. Here in this very speech is the doctrine of man. Elimelech means 'My God is King.' In that Hebrew name we have God's purpose for man. We're born to let God have supremacy in all things. Elimelech married Naomi which means 'Pleasure.' Man, in the garden did that very thing by obeying his own desires rather than God's, and it very quickly turned to Mara bitterness. These two sons 'Sickness' and 'Pining away' were the result. Yet man was stiffnecked because he went on stubbornly like Orpah - 'Stiffnecked.' Then came Ruth - 'Beautiful,' who obeyed God and through Boaz, the man of strength, we hear him redeeming all that was Elimelech's, Mahlon's, Chilion's, Ruth's and Naomi's. What a circle! -but it is not complete yet: watch.

Boaz marries Ruth and slowly the circle takes its last curve. Ruth, who is hailed as better than seven sons (the perfect family), bears a son whose name is Obed. The name is more than significant. What does it mean? Some render it servant; others render it worship, but both give the idea of humility and obedience. What, you ask me, do you mean by the fact that the circle is not complete? I mean just this. This amazing love story ends with a genealogy. Now, that in modern writing is a most unromantic way to end any story. Yet, if you look closely enough you will see that it could not be more romantic. For Boaz begat Obed, and Obed begat Jesse, and Jesse begat David. What is so amazing about that? David was - the King! What a circle from the first tragedy of Elimelech, 'My God is King' in famine and death to Obed, the servant to David - the King! As for God, His way is perfect, for in that very town centuries later David's greater Son came to redeem not only all that was Elimelech's, Mahlon's, Chilion's, Naomi's and Ruth, but to you and me and all men, women, boys and girls who will put their trust in Him.

Did we not say when we first set off on our stroll amidst alien corn that we would see that something beautiful always comes out of the tragic, if God is trusted. It is no different today. As you and I say goodbye, let me say just one final word.

Whether it be the unending tragedy of this island on which I live, the cancer that surrounds us, poverty, death, no matter what, God is not dead. He is always working out His purpose in Christ. He is a happy young person who rests at the Saviour's feet. Whom He loves, He chastens; the end product is the thing that matters. Ruth certainly was wise to say, 'Thy God shall be my God.' She may have seemed to her friends peculiar, but better a thousand times effective peculiarly than uneffective ordinariness. Her complete subordination to a single aim was absolute. No person who goes for that aim with singleheartedness can fail, God promises, repeat, promises, that 'them that honour Me, I will honour.'

Ruth's marriage to Boaz was God's doing. No more gleaning for Ruth - she now had the hand of the man who owned the whole field. It is my prayer that you, if you know not Christ, will no longer wander the world trying to glean a little here and there - but rather that you will put your hand in the hand of the One who owns it all. Again, if you do know Him, go and enjoy all the privileges that are yours - go to His storehouse, of which you are a joint heir in Christ, and see if he will not open the windows of heaven, and pour you out a blessing, that there shall not be room enough to receive it. It involves your all, but it ends far from gleaning alien corn. The end-it will explain. It ends in having - Him.

Will not the end explain
The crossed endeavour, earnest purpose foiled.
The strange bewilderment of good work spoiled,
The clinging weariness, the inward strain,
Will not the end explain?

Meanwhile He comforteth
Them that are losing patience. 'Tis His way:
But none can write the words they hear Him say
For men to read; only they know He saith
Sweet words, and comforteth.

Not that He doth explain
The mystery that baffleth; but a sense
Husheth the quiet heart, that far, far hence
Lieth a field set thick with golden grain
Wetted in seedling days by many a rain:
The end - it will explain.